Corporate Finance and
Capital Management for the
Chief Executive Officer
and Directors

Corporate Finance and Capital Management for the Chief Executive Officer and Directors

John F. Childs

PRENTICE-HALL, INC.   Englewood Cliffs, NJ

Prentice-Hall International, Inc., *London*
Prentice-Hall of Australia, Pty. Ltd., *Sydney*
Prentice-Hall of Canada, Ltd., *Toronto*
Prentice-Hall of India Private Ltd., *New Delhi*
Prentice-Hall of Japan, Inc., *Tokyo*
Whitehall Books, Ltd., *Wellington, New Zealand*
Prentice-Hall of Southeast Asia Pte. Ltd., *Singapore*

© 1979 by

John F. Childs

Library of Congress Cataloging in Publication Data

Childs, John Farnsworth.
   Corporate finance and capital management for the
chief executive officer and directors.

   Includes index.
   1. Corporations--Finance. 2. Capital investments.
I. Title.
HG4026.C52   658.1'5   79-10750
ISBN 0-13-174003-2

Printed in the United States of America

DEDICATION

This fifth book I also dedicate to my daughter. May her children be as fine as she is, and may they give her as much happiness as she has given me.

ABOUT THE AUTHOR

John F. Childs is widely known as an advisor, lecturer and writer on all phases of corporate finance for all types of corporations. He has worked in Wall Street for over 40 years, initially as a financial analyst with an investment banking firm. Subsequently, he joined a major New York bank where, as a Senior Vice President, he spent his time largely as an advisor to corporations on financial policy and capital management. He is now a senior officer of a leading investment banking firm.

Mr. Childs has been a corporate director and a director of a number of business associations.

His original book *Long-Term Financing* achieved 12 printings and acceptance as one of the most practical books in its field. He is also author of *Profit Goals and Capital Management* and *Earnings per Share and Management Decisions*. In 1976 he wrote the comprehensive book *Encyclopedia of Long-Term Finance and Capital Management* which combined all of his previous books with revised and much added content. All four books were published by Prentice Hall, Inc.

. This book includes some of the material from the *Encyclopedia of*

Long-Term Finanancing and Capital Management. Such portions are revised, summarized and supplemented so as to fulfill their specific purpose.

A WORD FROM THE AUTHOR

Finance and capital management are largely the job of the financial vice-president and other executives in charge of capital management. However, since capital is highly important to the success of most companies, you, the chief executive officer, have to approve the principal decisions. In order to do so you need to have appropriate goals for finance and capital management.

Directors also need similar goals in order to judge how their management team is handling the company.

This book is designed specifically to meet your needs and that of your directors.

The broad goals that you might have for your company are:

1. Assure that outside capital will be available when it is needed for expansion at a reasonable cost.
2. Produce a satisfactory return on capital.
3. Have a satisfactory price for your common stock.

To assure that these goals will be achieved and also to provide a means for you to monitor the progress of your company, there are three ratios which must be established. They are the basis for financial planning. They are:

1. The ratio of LONG-TERM DEBT TO TOTAL LONG-TERM CAPITAL.
2. The RETURN ON COMMON EQUITY BOOK VALUE WITH A SOUND DEBT RATIO.
3. The amount of EARNINGS THAT SHOULD BE PAID OUT IN DIVIDENDS.

The first three chapters show how proper ratios should be established for your company. Since they will be used to guide your company, you will want an in-depth understanding of them. While I have tried to make them as easy to digest as possible, they will require some concentration.

Chapter 4 explains *How These Three Ratios Circumscribe Your Company's Future*, and how they assure that other important ratios will be in line.

At times, you might wish that your stockholders would go away and leave you more time to concentrate on doing a good job for them. No chance! In fact they are getting more vocal. Is *Investor Relations* an obligation? Is it worthwhile? What part should you play? Who should be cultivated? These and other questions are answered in Chapter 5.

Earning per Share are bound to be on your mind. What do variations in earnings per share mean? This depends on what causes the variation. There are five ways that they grow, and this is explained in Chapter 6. For various reasons, you will wish to have some idea as to *What Your Stock Should Sell For*. This is also discussed in Chapter 6.

You may want to have a nodding acquaintance with many other things with which your financial vice-president will be concerned and may wish to discuss with you. Therefore, in Chapter 7 I will comment briefly on some of the additional *Things Your Financial Officer May Have to Think About*.

Finally, you may enjoy *A Summary of Finance and Capital Management* in a very few words in Chapter 8.

John F. Childs

Acknowledgments

To Jeff Parker for his careful reading of the final draft, to Dan Nobel for his help with the industry tables, and to Joan Russo for her cheerful secretarial help.

CONTENTS

Chapter 1

ASSURING THAT CAPITAL WILL BE AVAILABLE

YOUR COMPANY'S SOURCES OF CAPITAL

The first questions that may arise in your mind regarding capital are:

Where in my company does capital come from?
What amount is available?
What assurance do I have that it will be available?

There are four principal sources of capital which will show up in your company's statement of sources and uses of funds.

One source is developed from revenues in the income statement from:

1. *CASH FLOW* from non-cash expense items such as depreciation and from earnings retained after dividends.

Three sources are developed in the balance sheet from:

2. Liquidation or SALE OF ASSETS.
3. SHORT TERM BORROWINGS.
4. SALE OF LONG-TERM SECURITIES, such as bonds and stock.

Exhibit 1–1

Sources of Corporate Funds

Income Statement

Sales	$200
Operating expenses	171
Depreciation	6
Interest	2
Taxes	10
Total	$190
Net Income	$ 10
Common dividends	5
Retained earnings	$ 5

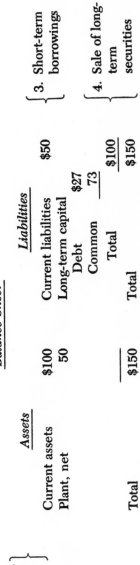

1. Cash flow

Non-cash expenses

Retained earnings

Balance Sheet

Assets		Liabilities	
Current assets	$100	Current liabilities	$50
Plant, net	50	Long-term capital	
		Debt	$27
		Common	73
		Total	$100
Total	$150	Total	$150

2. Sale of assets

3. Short-term borrowings

4. Sale of long-term securities

These four principal sources of capital are illustrated in Exhibit 1–1. The figures are reasonably representative of an industrial type of company.

Cash flow from the income statement is limited and varies with earnings; sale of assets is generally not a ready source of capital; short-term borrowings used for capital purposes have to be paid back.

These three sources of capital have to be taken into account in financial planning, but the open door that you should be able to count on for obtaining capital is from the sale of long-term securities. If your company has this ability, it will be able to meet maturing obligations and pursue expansion projects as they may arise.

BASIC TYPES OF SECURITIES

There are two basic types of long-term securities—debt and equity. Your first and most important ratio to establish in financial planning is the division of your company's long-term capital between debt and equity. There are many other types of securities, but they fall into either one of these two broad categories. Long-term debt should include short-term debt rolled over and not paid off seasonally and leases capitalized.

There are various ways to express the relationship of debt to equity; we will use long-term debt as a percent of total long-term capital. In Exhibit 1–1, it is 27% as follows:

Long-term capital	Amount	Percent
Debt	$ 27	27%
Common	73	73
Total	$100	100%

DEBT VS COMMON—LEVERAGE

With regard to the use of debt for raising capital, you may naturally think of the following three advantages of debt over common:

Interest saves taxes.

There is less immediate dilution of earnings per share.

When the capital is put to work earnings per share of common stock will show a greater increase.

For example, suppose the figures that applied to your company were as presented in Exhibit 1–2, which shows the effect of the sale of $10,000,000 debt vs $10,000,000 common. If you trace the figures through you will see that earnings per share are affected as follows:

		After Sale of Common	After Sale of Debt
Before Financing.. $6.00			
Immediate Dilution		$5.45	$5.80
After Capital is Put to Work		6.00	6.40

Thus, on the basis of our assumptions, the immediate dilution of earnings per share from the sale of common is from $6.00 to $5.45. Earnings would recover to $6.00 after the capital is put to work.

However, the Exhibit suggests that you should rely on debt for raising capital because the immediate dilution is less, $5.80 compared to $5.45. And also because earnings per share are greater when capital is put to work—$6.40 compared to $6.00. This is what is meant by the advantages of leverage.

These figures, however, do not tell all the story, and too much debt can ultimately lead to adverse results. How then can you decide what is an appropriate amount of debt?

GOALS FOR LONG-TERM CAPITAL

In the introduction, we suggested that you might have as a financial goal to assure that outside capital will be available when it is needed for expansion at a reasonable cost. We can expand this goal as a basis for determining the ratio of long-term debt to total long-term capital as follows:

Exhibit 1–2

**Illustration of the Effect of Financing
with Debt vs Common**

Part I
YOUR COMPANY BEFORE FINANCING

Book value of common	$100,000,000
Common shares	2,000,000
Net income for common	$ 12,000,000
Earnings per share	$ 6.00
Market price of common	$ 50.00
Return on common book value	12%

Part II
CAPITAL REQUIRED AND EXPECTED RETURN

New capital	$ 10,000,000
After tax return on new capital after it is put to work	12%

Part III
FINANCING

Debt at 8% interest	$ 10,000,000
or	
Common 200,000 Shares at $50 per share	$ 10,000,000

Part IV
EFFECT OF FINANCING WITH DEBT VS COMMON
(Assuming 50% tax rate)

	Earnings per Share	
Before financing	$6.00	
	After Sale of common	*After Sale of debt*
Immediate dilution	$5.45	$5.80
After capital is put to work	$6.00	$6.40

1. ASSURE YOUR COMPANY'S ABILITY TO RAISE CAP-
    ITAL AT ALL TIMES.

    This means during both favorable and unfavorable condi-
    tions when your company's earnings are poor and security
    markets are adverse.

2. ASSURE YOUR COMPANY'S ABILITY TO RAISE
    CAPITAL AT ALL TIMES WITHOUT STRAINING
    ITS CREDIT.

    Once a company's credit is strained, it is a long, costly and
    restricting operation to restore sound credit.

3. RAISE CAPITAL UNDER ALL CONDITIONS AT THE
    LEAST COST SO THAT YOUR COMPANY CAN MEET
    COMPETITIVE PRICES AND PRODUCE A SATIS-
    FACTORY RETURN TO THE STOCKHOLDERS IN
    THE LONG RUN.

    This means avoiding:

    a. High rates for senior capital.
    b. Unduly restrictive terms in senior securities.
    c. Excessive rates on junior securities or including costly
        "kickers" in the form of incentive securities such as
        convertibles and warrants.
    d. Selling common stock when the price is depressed.
    e. Adding unnecessary risk to the common stock so that
        investors require a high return.

4. ASSURE THAT DIVIDENDS WILL NOT HAVE TO BE
    CUT FOR FINANCIAL REASONS.

5. HAVE A GOOD QUALITY COMMON STOCK WHICH
    WILL HELP REDUCE ERRATIC MARKET SWINGS.

    Such a stock should have a regular gradual increase in
    earnings per share as the common stock investment in-
    creases through retained earnings. With a stable price-
    earnings ratio, there should be long-range price apprecia-

tion. Increase in earnings per share from retained earnings will be explained subsequently.

These five objectives call for the use of debt to the extent appropriate, because of the advantages of debt. However, if debt is increased past a certain point these objectives cannot be achieved. We will now explain how to establish an appropriate debt ratio.

THE ATMOSPHERE YOU HAVE TO WORK IN

Financial policy can not be tested on the basis that everything will always be rosy. The real test comes when a company runs into unfavorable earnings and the stock market is unreceptive to new capital.

An adverse period cannot be foreseen by management because of the inability to forecast more than a limited number of years ahead with any degree of certainty. A company may encounter one or more of four difficulties:

1. Economy problems, including recession and inflation.
2. Security market crisis.
3. Industry problems.
4. Company problems.

In determining financial policy, a company should allow for the possibility of any one or more of these difficulties happening some time in the unforeseeable future.

The key to a company's ability to raise capital at all times and under all conditions is its ability to sell debt. Debt can practically always be sold if a company keeps its capital structure in order without too much leverage when its earnings are satisfactory.

INFLEXIBILITY OF CAPITAL STRUCTURE

Under favorable conditions, any fool can go into debt to increase leverage and it can be done very quickly. However, capital structure is flexible in only one direction; it is easy to get into debt but all of the ways to correct an excessive debt ratio are arduous:

1. Building up equity from retained earnings is a slow process.
2. Reducing debt from internal cash generation may also be a slow process.
3. Sale of common to build up equity depends on favorable market conditions.
4. If the proceeds from the sale of common are used to pay off debt, it generally results in dilution of earnings per share.
5. Sale of assets to pay off debt is generally not available.

Investors require a long record of good earnings and sound financing after a company's credit has been strained before they will accept improvement. They want proof that management will continue to follow a sound policy. It may take from five to ten years to correct a poor financial position and gain acceptance. This is a tedious and costly process and may restrict a company's ability to grow.

THE RISK OF BUSINESS AFFECTS AMOUNT OF DEBT

There are three basic risks in a company.

1. THE RISK OF THE BUSINESS ITSELF.
   For example, an industrial company is more risky than an electric utility company.

2. A FINANCIAL RISK WHICH IS ADDED BY MAN-
   AGEMENT INCREASING THE DEBT RATIO TOO
   FAR.

   As debt is added past a certain point, financing becomes
   difficult, and the quality of all the securities of a company
   becomes speculative. This results in an increase in the cost
   of debt. Since the common is junior to the debt, it too must
   have risk added to it, and this increases the return that
   stockholders' require. Thus, the total return required by
   investors is increased as debt is added past a certain point.

3. A CREDIBILITY GAP OR INVESTOR RELATIONS
   RISK, WHEN MANAGEMENT DOES NOT TELL THE
   TRUTH OR FAILS TO GIVE OUT ADEQUATE IN-
   FORMATION.

   This third risk will be discussed in Chapter 5.

Management cannot change the risk of a business unless it
changes the business itself. This is not to say that the characteristics
of a business may not change over time. However, at any one time,
the risk will depend on the nature of the business.

Risk of a business is assessed in terms of the possible amplitude of
variations likely to occur in its earnings. The extent of risk may be
revealed in the past earnings, but this is not necessarily so. There
may be inherent risks due to the nature of the business which have
not shown up in past earnings.

Potential risk, unrecorded in historical earnings, must be assessed from a study of all the factors which may affect risk, such as
the make-up of sales, potential competition, expenses which may
increase, technical problems, obsolescence, etc. For example, suppose that a company manufacturing auto parts and selling all its
output to one automobile company has had a good earnings record
for ten years. Past earnings would tend to indicate little risk. But the
risk might be substantial because of the dependence on one cus-
tomer.

ESTABLISHING A POLICY FOR YOUR COMPANY

Most companies have sufficient stability to use debt up to a certain point without adding a significant financial risk. Your company should have a financial policy which will use leverage up to the point that a financial risk is not added.

Risk may vary widely from industry to industry and affect the use of debt as shown in Exhibit 1–3. Also, there may be differences in risk for companies within an industry so that the appropriate debt ratio will vary from company to company. Principles of finance are generally the same for all types of companies; their application will differ depending on the nature of the business as it affects risk and special financing needs.

The question we are seeking to answer is: How can you establish a policy for your company's long-term capital which will use leverage properly and achieve the five goals? To repeat, the goals are:

1. Ability to raise capital at all times.
2. Ability to raise capital without straining credit.
3. Raise capital at the lowest cost.
4. Assure no dividend cuts for financial reasons.
5. Have a good quality common stock.

In other words, how much debt can your company use without adding a financial risk and maintain financial flexiblity? Is 25% right or should it be higher or lower? The answer is not easy because there are no ready pegs on which to hang your hat.

QUALITY OF SECURITIES—THE KEY TO LONG-TERM CAPITAL DETERMINATION

An individual's ability to obtain capital and the terms and price he will have to pay depend on his earnings, his assests and the amount to which he has gone into hock. Has he got a good steady salary?

Exhibit 1–3

Financial Ratios for Various Types
of Businesses

1977

	All Manufacturing Companies[1]	Electric Utility Companies[2]	Finance Companies[3]	All Insured U.S. Commercial Banks[4]
Long-term capital				
Debt	25%	51%	83%	93%
Equity	75	49	17	7
Total	100%	100%	100%	100%
Times fixed charges earned before income taxes	6.8x	2.9x[5]	1.7x	—
Cash flow as a percent of long-term debt	65%	14%	—	—
Return on average common equity	14.3%	11.4%	15.2%	11.7%

[1]Quarterly Financial Report for Manufacturing Corporations, Federal Trade Commission.
[2]Edison Electric Institute Statistical Year Book.
[3]Average of Avco Financial Services, Inc. and Dial Financial Corporation.
[4]Federal Deposit Insurance Corporation Annual Report. Long-term capital is represented by total liabilities.
[5]Including AFDC as other income.

Does he have liquid assests? Does he borrow sensibly? These questions might be put in another way: Is his credit excellent, fair or poor quality?

The same idea applies to a company in determining the amount of debt it should have, that is, what should be the quality of its credit?

The quality of credit determines your company's ability to sell securities and the price and terms on which they can be sold. A company with good credit will be able to do some form of financing even under adverse conditions; it will have financial flexibility.

We first think of credit quality in terms of a company's debt securities. As we have said, the quality of a company's debt affects the quality of the equity since the equity is in a junior position. It is impossible to have a low quality debt and a high grade equity.

In extremes, we might think of a company's debt as being of such good quality that it is like a government bond; in other words, no one would question its quality. At the other extreme would be a company with very poor credit so that there is concern about the company's ability to pay its interest and principal. Between these two extremes are various gradations of quality ranging from good to fair to speculative.

In order to talk about quality, it is handy to have symbols for the various grades. We could use 1st, 2nd, 3rd, etc, or A, B, C, etc. Better yet, we have a ready-made bond rating system provided by the rating agencies. The rating agencies are Moody's Investors Service Inc., Standard & Poor's Corporation, and Fitch Investor's Service Inc. They use symbols such as AAA, AA, A, BBB, BB, etc. They rate other securities such as preferred stocks and commercial paper, but for our present purpose we are interested in bond ratings.

Some people are critical of these ratings. They claim that the ratings are not accurate and that a company should not be a slave to ratings because the rating agencies are only an isolated part of the financial scene. However, a company cannot avoid having its financial position being thought of in terms of the quality rating for its bonds. A company may sell a bond privately and thus avoid a rating, because many privately offered bonds are not rated. However, financial experts will evaluate its debt in much the same way as the rating agency analysts, and will undoubtedly think of its quality in terms of the bond rating. Thus, bond ratings are a part of the language of finance.

What quality ratings should you try to achieve in establishing a financial policy? The BB rating is definitely eliminated. Such bonds have an uncertain future. Generally, they can only be sold in favorable markets. Investors will require a relatively high interest rate and may require kickers. A company might have to cut its dividend.

The BBB rating is one step better and under ordinary conditions a company with such a bond rating can finance. But bonds with that quality do contain some speculative elements and are not high grade.

Therefore, we are left with three ratings which would satisfy our goals: AAA, AA, and A.

A company with an AAA rating is the *creme de la creme*. It has all kinds of financial strength. For this reason the rating agencies reserve the AAA rating for a few very choice, large companies. The stocks of such companies are the bluest of blue chip.

Is AAA stronger than necessary? This is debatable. However, companies in this category are generally very large, and when they offer securities the amounts are large. The AAA rating puts them in good position to appeal to a broad group of investors to absorb large security offerings. Furthermore, for companies with a continuous need to attract large amounts of capital under all economic conditions, the AAA rating gives financial flexibility in adverse periods when new money may otherwise be unavailable.

The AA rating is excellent quality. A company with AA rated bonds only fails to be AAA because it has some characteristics which prevent it from being perfect. Only large companies receive an AA bond rating. Such companies can achieve an AA rating and have a reasonable portion of their long-term capital in the form of debt. A company of this type would be in a strong position to fulfill the five goals we have suggested for capital structure determination. Therefore, such a company would do well to have AA as its measure of quality.

Most companies, particularly in the industrial field, can only have their bonds rated A and have an opportunity to use a reasonable amount of debt. Thus, their borrowing ability would be highly restricted by trying to do better than A. They will have to settle for A as their goal.

FINANCIAL FLEXIBILITY—BORROWING RESERVE AND FINANCIAL INSURANCE

We have mentioned the term financial flexibility. A company with well-rated debt has financial strength because it has financial flexibility. We can use two terms to describe financial flexibility: borrowing reserve and financial insurance.

A company's debt ratio can vary within certain limits for a limited period of time without losing its bond rating. Borrowing reserve refers to this limited ability to increase long-term debt.

Financial insurance refers to the maintenance of adequate quality so that if a company's bond rating slips it will still have respectability. AAA and AA provide strong financial insurance. Grade A doesn't provide financial insurance because if the bond rating slips it falls into the inadequate category of BBB.

A summary of debt quality for capital structure determination is given in Exhibit 1–4.

Before we leave this section, a word about companies which have no debt whatsoever, even though they could have some debt with a good quality rating. On the basis of the above discussion, it would appear that companies with only common are being overly conservative. However, it is difficult to criticize them too severely. They have a built-in reserve which may come in handy; it is certainly worth something. It may be an advantage in this highly competitive world when companies find themselves in trouble and need to resort to large borrowings in a hurry. Such companies could maintain their dividend come hell or high water. In a sense, it may be said that their stocks have some of the investment attributes of senior securities. Most companies in this position are companies which have not needed to sell securities to raise outside capital. If they did need outside capital, it would be uneconomical not to use debt.

Exhibit 1–4

Summary of Debt Quality for
Capital Structure Determination

Bond
Rating

AAA	Unquestionable financial strength. Only a few companies can obtain this rating.
AA	High quality. Provides real financial strength. Only large companies can obtain this rating and be able to use a significant amount of debt. For such companies this rating is worth achieving. Provides financial insurance.
A	Fair quality. This is the best rating that most companies, particularly industrials, can achieve. It is lacking in financial insurance.
BBB	Inadequate quality.
BB	Poor quality.

QUALITY TRANSLATED INTO DEBT RATIO

Having determined the bond rating you desire for your senior debt, which will assure your ability to meet your financial goals, the next step is to translate that rating into a ratio of long-term debt to total long-term capital. That is the job of your financial vice-president. However, in order for you to know how he will have to proceed we will describe the process briefly.

A statistical comparison is made with similar companies which have rated bonds. This will include all of the financial ratios which are used to depict the quality of the bonds for the type of company. Such an analysis will include a complete review of the company's financial statements and all the factors which affect a company's earning power and variability.

The two most fundamental ratios are long-term debt as a percent of total long-term capital and the number of times interest charges are earned. It is primarily earnings, their amount, volatility and danger of decrease which make for the quality of bond. Therefore, the number of times interest is earned will weigh most heavily in the study. A company with low debt may have a good looking balance sheet, but if it is a poor earner, its debt will have poor quality.

The nature of a company's assets in terms of their liquidity may be important. Other things being equal, a company with a large part of its assets consisting of special types of plant and equipment, which are not readily salable, is less attractive to a lender then a company with liquid types of assets.

Once the figures have been arrayed in a statisitical comparison and studied carefully, then judgment has to be applied in coming to a conclusion as to how much long-term debt your company can carry, as compared with the other companies, and receive a particular rating.

Your financial vice-president should keep such a statistical study up-to-date and observe how the ratios and ratings change. This will help him understand how changes in your company may affect its debt quality.

MAXIMUM DEBT RATIO—WITH GOOD CREDIT

In our approach to establishing a debt ratio as a key for financial planning, we have talked about average debt ratio. An average presupposes fluctuations below and above the average.

We have pointed out that managements generally favor the use of debt and avoid selling common stock like the plague. If a company's debt ratio is at the average and a company needs to raise outside capital, management will naturally turn to debt. There is nothing wrong with this reasoning, but what is wrong is where it leads. Subsequently, if more outside capital is needed, the urge will be to use debt again.

Therefore, as an additional key for financial planning, it is necessary to define the maximum debt ratio. The maximum debt ratio should act as a red light which will alert management to the need for equity and prevent a drift too far in the wrong direction. There is no need to establish a minimum debt ratio; it represents no problem in financial planning.

How far away from the average can the maximum extend and for how long? This has to be within limits so as to maintain the quality rating that has been established as your company's goal. The extent of variation will depend on the ability of your company to get back to the average and how long it will take; this will be affected by your company's cash flow.

The maximum we have talked about is a maximum with good credit and is not to be confused with the maximum the company can borrow. The maximum the company can borrow will result in a debt ratio which will produce poor quality credit.

Thus, an average debt ratio and a maximum debt ratio which will provide a good quality debt are essential tools for financial planning. And the difference between the average debt ratio and maximum debt ratio provides what we have described as borrowing reserve.

Because of the importance of earnings on the quality of debt, another ratio which should be established is the minimum coverage of interest charges that can occur for a limited period of time and still maintain a specific bond rating. This, in effect, corresponds to the maximum debt ratio.

BREAKING UP A COMPANY
FOR DEBT RATIO DETERMINATION

For most companies, debt capacity is determined by looking at the company as a whole. For example, the assets of most manufacturing companies consist of plant and current assets, including receivables which are not interest bearing. The plant and receivables are an integral part of the whole operation. Nothing would be gained by breaking up the company into parts and deciding how much mortgage debt the plant could carry and how much could be borrowed on the receivables.

There are some exceptions when the parts of the company are really divisible. For example, a department store is in three businesses; receivables financing, real estate and merchandising. The receivables are interest bearing and could be segregated in a separate finance company. The real estate is fairly general purpose and also could be placed in a separate company. To determine an overall debt ratio for the enterprise, appropriate debt ratios can be applied to these segments and then weighted by the capital employed. Leases play an important part in most retailing businesses and they should all be capitalized.

SMALL COMPANIES—USE BOND RATING
APPROACH INDIRECTLY

Size of company affects the risk in the eyes of investors. A small company is generally more vulnerable to factors adversely affecting sales and expenses. Management tends to be dependent on a single person or a few key people.

Since risk is greater for small companies, they will receive low bond ratings even though they have a small amount of debt. They will have to pay higher interest rates than a large company, regardless of their debt ratio. Relying on bond ratings as a guide to debt ratio would restrict a small company's use of debt. Therefore, you cannot use bond ratings directly in establishing an average and maximum debt ratio for a small company.

This may seem illogical and that we are abandoning our basic approach to quality. Not so. We will still use quality, but think in terms of the rating the company would receive if it were large. It should establish an average and maximum debt ratio on this basis.

For example, if you strived for an A rating, assuming your company were large, it would produce what might be termed a fair credit standing for a small company. The ratios would be sufficiently in line so that buyers of debt would feel comfortable and commerical bankers would not hesitate to lend short term funds.

What is small depends to some extent on the nature of the business. In general, the dividing line may be $100 million of common equity capital.

PRIVATELY OWNED COMPANIES

The owner of a private company can take whatever risk he chooses. Furthermore, a privately owned company, unlike a publicly owned company, is not dependent on the volatility of the stock market and on having to present a good earnings picture to public investors. The slow acceptance of improved credit standing by stockholders, which occurs in a publicly owned company, does not exist in a privately owned company. Owners of a private company can evaluate the situation based on their current intimate knowledge of the company. Therefore, a privately owned company may be able to have a higher debt ratio and be more flexible than a publicly owned company, providing, of course, the owners have more of their own money to dump in if they encounter adversity.

On the other hand, if the owners have no extra capital, a privately owned company is less flexible than a publicly owned company. Then, its only source of outside capital is through debt financing, and, if its capital needs are large, it may get into debt up to the hilt rather quickly.

If a privately owned company intends to go public in a few years, it should do financial planning as though it were publicly owned in order to prepare itself for the day it comes out of its shell. It will be judged on its past financials and it cannot go back and change them when the company decides to go public.

ADHERENCE TO PROPER FINANCIAL POLICY
NOT ALWAYS POSSIBLE

When a new company is started, the investors who put in the seed money may not have enough capital to provide adequate equity. Furthermore, they may be willing to take the risk of high debt ratio.

A mature company may run into difficulties and lose its rating so that its financial position becomes weak. There are many companies with BBB and BB rated debt. While such situations are not ideal, a company cannot abandon ship. It will have to do the best it can under the circumstances. However, management should have a plan to gradually reach the proper goal. If it has no plan, it may drift in the wrong direction and run a chance of getting into financial trouble.

FALSE APPROACHES TO DEBT VS. COMMON

Your financial vice-president should be familiar with other approaches that are sometimes suggested as ways to determine the use of debt vs. common. We summarize two:

Spread in Yield Between Bond Ratings

There is a superficial approach to financial policy which says that there is relatively little cost differential between AA, A, and BBB bonds, and the added debt which can be obtained with BBB bonds more than offsets the small added cost.

The spread in yield between ratings widens as the ratings decrease in quality. It will vary from time to time depending upon market conditions. The spread may not be too significant in a favorable bond market, but it may be material in a financial crunch.

However, the added interest cost is only a small part of the disadvantage of too much debt and a low rating. As debt is increased, the quality of the debt decreases, but more important, the quality of the junior securities and the common decrease and the total return investors require on all securities rises. Thus, the addition of debt past the point of good credit may increase the total burden of capital in the long run.

Furthermore, as we have explained throughout this chapter, there are many other important considerations in determining long-range financial policy which favor a company having a good quality rating for its debt.

Cash Flow

Another false approach to determine the amount of debt is the school that suggests the use of cash flow. This approach may sound plausible because cash flow can be used for debt repayment.

However, this theory is unsound for a number of reasons. Cash flow shows the ability of a company to repay debt, but not necessarily its ability to raise new capital. A company with a good cash flow because of large non-cash items such as high depreciation, will not have financial strength if it does not have good earnings. Such a company is more of a liquidating proposition, and most lenders do not want to do business with that type of company. A company, to have a good future, must have the ability to earn. It is earning power after depreciation which should carry the most weight in determining the quality of securities. Without earnings, a company will eventually be unable to raise common equity, and a strong equity is one of the bases for financial strength. Furthermore, the cash flow approach does not work for certain types of companies. For example, cash flow could not be used to determine debt capacity of a bank. A bank is loaded with cash or equivalents. Nor could cash flow be used to determine the debt capacity of an electric utility. An electric utility has only a small cash flow relative to its capital requirements. Its bonds generally have no cash sinking fund; the stability of earnings in the past have permitted it to use a large amount of debt which is repaid at maturity with another debt issue.

We are not suggesting that cash flow can be disregarded in determining debt capacity. On the contrary, it is a factor to consider, and in some industries it may be quite important, but earning power is dominant. As we previously mentioned, cash flow may be more important in determining the spread between the average and maximum debt ratio.

WINDOW DRESSING YOUR BALANCE SHEET—A FREE LUNCH?

There may be financial maneuvers which you can execute which will build up your stated amount of equity. For example, if you have an undervalued asset you may be able to sell it for more than its stated book value and lease it back. The after-tax increase in value may be transferred to the capital stock account. Thus, you have provided more book keeping equity. However, you haven't improved your company's earnings and you have taken on more debt in the form of lease payments. In fact, you may have taken on a high cost form of debt.

Another example is the exchange of a low coupon preferred stock, selling at a discount from its stated value, for a high coupon preferred. The discount may be transferred to common equity. However, this is done at a cost, because you have to offer the existing preferred stockholders a premium in terms of more dividends to induce them to make the exchange.

It is earnings that count and more equity without earnings isn't worth much. In other words, leverage, or the use of senior securities, shows up in the balance sheet, but the important effect of leverage is measured by the burden on earnings of charges on senior securities. Therefore, such window dressing operations should be approached with caution.

POLICIES FOLLOWED BY COMPANIES

Before we summarize this chapter, we will take a look at what policies companies follow.

As we explained, size is very important in bond ratings, and for this reason many companies are limited in the rating they can achieve. And adverse circumstances may prevent some companies from achieving the goal that they would like to have. These facts have to be kept in mind when viewing data on bond ratings.

In Exhibit 1–5 is shown the ratings on publicly held senior debt by Moody's Investors Service Inc. and Standard & Poor's Corporation for the 50 largest industrial companies with sales of $4 billion and over and the 500 largest companies with sales over $350 million.

These figures show the preponderance of companies in the higher rating categories. For example, the figures for Moody's Investors Service, Inc. show that for the largest companies, 62% are Aa or higher and 92% are A or higher. For the 500 largest companies, 31% are Aa or higher and 76% are A or higher. Figures for Standard and Poor's Corporation are similar.

SUMMARY

In summary, the aim in financial policy should be to make it possible for a company to raise whatever capital is needed so it can pursue any capital investments management deems appropriate. It should be able to finance at its own choosing and not be forced into

Exhibit 1–5

Bond Ratings of Senior Debt of Industrial Companies

Part I
Moody's Investors Service, Inc.

	50 Largest Companies with Sales of $4 billion and over		500 Largest Companies with Sales over $350 million	
	Number	Percent	Number	Percent
Aaa	16	34%	22	8%
Aa	13	28	62	23
A	14	30	122	45
Lower Rating	4	8	65	24
Total Rated	47	100%	271	100%
Not Rated[1]	3		229	
Total	50		500	

Part II
Standard and Poor's Corporation

	50 Largest Companies with Sales of $4 billion and over		500 Largest Companies Sales over $350 million	
	Number	Percent	Number	Percent
AAA	16	34%	22	8%
AA	14	30	60	23
A	12	25	119	46
Lower Rating	5	11	61	23
Total Rated	47	100%	262	100%
Not Rated[1]	3		238	
Total	50		500	

[1]Not rated because companies have no debt or because debt is privately held. Privately held debt may not be rated, or if it is rated, the ratings are generally not made public.

the sale of long-term securities at the mercy of security markets at rates and terms dictated by security buyers.

Debt is cheaper than other types of securities and interest is deductible for tax purposes. While leverage works for you on the upswing, it may work against you on the downswing. Leverage itself is not bad; our economy is based on the use of debt by both companies and individuals. The important point is to use it within range which will be to your company's benefit over the long run even if adversity is experienced. This requires a rating on senior debt no lower than A grade, and preferably AA if a company is large and strong enough to permit it adequate access to the debt market.

Your part in this policy matter is to formulate with your financial vice-president the bond rating that your company should achieve as a goal. If your company has that rating at present, you should know what financing can be done in the future and still maintain that rating. If you have to improve your company's rating, you should know how this will be accomplished, how long it will take and the restraints that this may require on capital expenditures.

Chapter 2

THE EARNINGS
YOU HAVE TO ACHIEVE

The purpose of profits is threefold:

1. TO REWARD INVESTORS WHO SUPPLY THE CAPI-
   TAL.
2. TO ACT AS A GUIDE IN ALLOCATING CAPITAL.
3. TO ACT AS AN INCENTIVE.

As far as financing and capital management are concerned, you
will be interested in the first two categories in managing your
company.

Questions you might have in this regard are:

How do I measure my company's performance?
What should my company achieve, that is, what is breakeven,
what is good and what is excellent?
How do I use profits in capital management decisions?

HOW DO YOU MEASURE YOUR PERFORMANCE?

You will be interested in the dollar amount and changes in your company's income. However, profits have to be measured in relation to some base. Percent of sales is a significant figure, but the best measure is in relation to the investment required to produce the profits.

We have said that one of the three ratios to follow in monitoring your company's progress is return on your stockholders' investment, providing your company has the appropriate capital structure. There are other bases on which to measure return on investment which follow from return on stockholders' investment; we will discuss them subsequently.

You may feel uneasy about return on your stockholders' investment. Earnings may be over or understated. And the reported amount of common equity may not be realisitc because of intangibles, or undervalued assets. These factors have to be kept in mind.

However, the fact is that the return on the investment the stockholders made in your company is the ultimate financial result. And retained earnings currently add to book value. An investor cannot recoup his past investment and current additional investment if the company does not earn enough so that the stock will sell at or above book value.

There are some people, particularly in the investment community, who stress cash flow rather than earnings. Cash flow is important from the investors' point of view. However, management must pay attention to profits. Cash flow represents both the return of capital and return on capital; management has to distinguish between the two.

WHAT SHOULD YOU ACHIEVE?

For your company to break-even, it must cover all costs. Costs should include earnings sufficient to compensate providers of capital fairly.

Part of your capital is borrowed capital. The interest rate you have to pay for that capital is relatively easy to determine.

The problem to solve is what rate of return you should earn on that part of your capital represented by the stockholders' investment.

Some of your stockholders' investment has been obtained internally from retained earnings. Retained earnings should earn the same rate as stockholders' investment raised through the sale of stock. If you do not treat retained earnings the same, stockholders should expect you to pay out the earnings in dividends and give them a choice as to whether to reinvest.

We have to decide what rate of return is just enough to induce investors to provide the capital.

The required rate must be measured in the marketplace because that is where you raise capital. On the other hand, your company's performance is measured on the stockholders' investment. For this reason, confusion may arise and we first have to eliminate this confusion.

RELATIONSHIP BETWEEN RETURN ON COMMON MARKET PRICE AND RETURN ON STOCKHOLDERS' INVESTMENT

How do the two rates tie together—one based on the market price and the other based on your company's investment.

To explain the relationship, we will use a simple example. Assume that a company's invested capital consists of one share of stock amounting to $100. The company earns $13, or 13% on the investment. Also assume that it pays out all of its earnings in dividends. Investors purchasing the stock will receive a $13 dividend. If investors require a 13% return, then the market price of the stock will be $100.

Assume another circumstance: instead of earning $13, the company earns 50% more than $13 or $19.50 and pays out all of its earnings in dividends. If investors want a 13% return, the market price of the stock would be $150 since $150 divided into $19.50 is 13%.

And further assume that the company earns 50% less than $13 or only $6.50. If investors want a 13% return, the market price of the stock would be $50, since $50 divided into $6.50 is 13%.

Once an investor has bought a new share of stock or the company has retained earnings, the investor can only get his money back by sale of stock in the market. If the company earns the minimum return that investors require to induce them to put up the capital, then the market price will be equal to the investment. If the company earns more than the minimum return investors require, the stock will sell above the investment. If the company earns less than the minimum return investors require, the stock will sell below the investment.

Thus, we obtain the return investors require on the basis of market price and measure the results by the return on book value. In order for investors to get their investment back by sale of stock in the market, the company must earn at least the minimum return that investors require on the market price.

We have assumed a very simple example. The real world is more complicated because companies don't pay out all their earnings in dividends, and stocks sell on what investors expect the company will earn, not on what the company has earned. However, these added complications don't change the idea we have illustrated.

WHAT IS MEANT BY THE MINIMUM RATE OF RETURN REQUIRED BY INVESTORS?

We will use two examples to explain what is meant by the minimum rate of return required on common investment.

As a first example, we ask you to give your answer to the question presented in Exhibit 2–1 regarding the return on common equity.

Exhibit 2-1

Your Thoughts on Minimum Common
Stock Return as an Investor

You have a deposit in a savings bank which is guaranteed by the F.D.I.C.—	$10,000 at 5% interest
You want to withdraw the $10,000 from the savings bank and make an investment in the securities market. You have a choice:	
1. Good grade bonds	$10,000 at 8% interest
2. Good grade common stock	$10,000
What total return on the common stock, from dividend yield and market appreciation combined, would be just enough to induce you to buy the common stock rather than the bonds.	_____%

It is interesting to ask this question of a group of people. You will receive some widely varying answers because each person will have different investment objectives. Consequently, people may require different returns for a particular risk. However, the average figures obtained from various groups of people are relatively close.

The answer to this question should indicate that there is a minimum return required to induce investors to provide common stock capital, because they have alternative ways to invest money.

Now we turn to our second example. As we explained in Chapter 1, there are two basic types of securities, debt and common equity. Let's assume that your company has a capital structure about the same as the average for all manufacturing companies, which is approximately as follows:

Debt	$27
Common equity	73
Total	$100

If the interest rate were 8% on the debt, your company would have to pay investors $2.16 in interest.

There is no contractual obligation to earn anything on the common stock. However, it is interesting to recast this long-term capital and replace all but 1% of the common stock with debt. This results in an obligation to pay the interest. We will use junior debt to replace $72 of common stock. It is difficult to say what interest rate might be required to make the junior debt marketable, because the total capital would be so debt heavy. However, if we use a minimum figure of 13%, then the company's requirements to pay the suppliers of capital would be as shown below, without allowing anything for the 1% of common stock.

	Amount	Interest Rate	Interest
Debt	$27	8%	$2.16
Junior Debt	72	13	9.36
Common equity	1	0	0.00
Total	$100		$11.52

Now the company would have to pay investors 11.52% on the $100. Merely changing the junior debt back to common should not relieve the company of its obligation to compensate the investors fairly for the capital they provide.

Because the management has no contractual obligation to earn a fixed return on its common equity, it can abuse its stockholders almost indefinitely. It can invest various sources of capital, such as funds resulting from sale of assets, funds obtained from borrowings, etc., without compensating stockholders fairly. This situation would be quickly rectified if either of the two following propositions occurred:

1. Each year all company funds had to be returned to your stockholders and you had to request your stockholders to give the funds back to your company.

2. Long-term capital was all in the form of debt as we illustrated above.

Of course, neither of these approaches is practical, but they help
to reinforce the point that there is a minimum return which a
company should earn on its common equity in order to compensate
investors. This is referred to as the cost rate for common. In other
words, all types of capital have a cost: for bonds it is the interest rate,
and for common stock it is the minimum return required by investors.

This basic concept obviously has significance to common stockholders. It also has significance for our competitive free market
economy. Since there is a limited amount of capital, it must be
allocated correctly. This statement may call for some explanation. In
order to protect the consumers, competition is supposed to drive
prices down to the point where all costs are covered. And all costs
should include the cost of all types of capital.

When a company decides that a product should be produced, it
has to consider whether there is a need. And whether there is a need
has to be tested by an affirmative answer to the question: will there
be sufficient revenues from sales to cover all costs, including the cost
of all types of capital? If revenues are not sufficient, then the
consumers do not want the product enough to justify its production.
The consumers would be saying, through the pricing mechanism,
that capital would be wasted. That capital should be used to produce
something more useful for which consumers would be willing to pay
a price to cover all cost. This is the framework within which management should make decisions.

As a matter of fact, the suggestion has been made that every
company should include in its income statement an amount to cover
the common cost for its stockholders' investment; profits would
represent any excess. If a company didn't earn the common cost, it
would show a loss. The idea is excellent and would be a good

discipline for management, but it is not practical for a number of reasons which we will not go into here.

Now we will try to quantify the cost rate of common.

THE COMMON COST RATE

In the previous discussion, we have assumed a rate of 13% as the cost rate for your common stock. Is it a reasonable figure?

This is a difficult question to answer with all necessary proof. However, we assume that you will not want a technical answer, but merely an idea of its general magnitude.

We can start with the obvious statement that the rate for common cost must be higher than the interest rate on a company's bonds. The common is in a more risky position; this bondholder has a first claim.

Much work has been done on the cost of common stock. When interest rates were lower it was generally accepted that a cost rate was around 11% for a large well situated company with a sound capital structure. Today, the common cost should be higher with interest rates having increased to over 8%.

In Exhibit 2–1, we asked you what return would be just sufficient to induce you to purchase a good grade common stock rather than a good grade bond yielding 8%?

If you could make a survey of all investors interested in your company's stock and get an answer to this question, you would have the figure for the cost rate for your common. Obviously, such a survey is impractical.

One interesting set of figures to look at is the return earned on common stock investment by industry as a whole. It is some indication of the common cost rate for the following reason:

We said competition should drive prices down to the point where

*all costs are covered, including the cost of capital. If our free
enterprise system works properly and prices are driven down to the
point where all costs are covered, then what all competitive industry
earns on its common investment may approximate the common cost
rate.*

This statement does not apply to the return earned by a single
company or even groups of companies, because they may earn more
or less than the common cost rate. Furthermore, figures for all
industry should be looked at over a number of years because of the
effect of variations in business activity.

In Exhibit 2–2, Part I is shown what all manufacturing companies
earned on common equity in the last 10 years, and in Part II is
shown a graph of the returns earned on the Fortune 500 companies
in 1977.

The figures in Part I for all manufacturing companies suggest a
common cost of 11% for the past, when interest rates were lower, and a
more current figure of about 13%. The median figure of the Fortune 500
in Part II also confirms this figure. However, don't be surprised if
experts in this field suggest a higher figure under special circumstances.

You might ask whether our figure of 13% takes into account the effect
of inflation. Supposedly yes, because the rate should be based on the
market where you raise capital, and the market has to evaluate the effect
of inflation. Whether it does it correctly is not the point. A company has
to accept the market cost for both its debt and its equity.

Now you may ask to what type of company does this figure apply?

For a large well-situated company with good quality securities,
that is, with bonds rated at least A grade, approximately the same
general rate can be used for the common regardless of type of
company. That statement may jar you. The reason for this statement
is the fact that variations in debt ratio should offset differences of risk
between types of companies. This is illustrated in the figures included in Exhibit 2–3 in the previous chapter. That exhibit showed

Exhibit 2–2
Returns on Common Equity
Part I
RETURN ON AVERAGE EQUITY FOR ALL MANUFACTURING COMPANIES

(Quarterly Financial Report for Manufacturing Corporations, Federal Trade Commission. Figures for preferred are included with common equity, but the amount of preferred is relatively small)

1977	1976	1975	1974	1973	1972	1971	1970	1969	1968
14.3%	14.1%	11.5%	15.1%	13.3%	10.7%	9.7%	9.4%	11.7%	12.2%

Average 1973–77—13.7%   Average 1968–72—10.7%

Part II
RETURN ON YEAR-END EQUITY

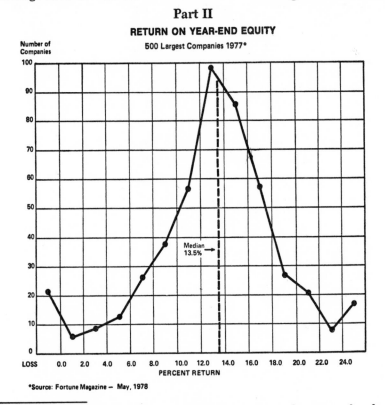

*Source: Fortune Magazine — May, 1978

---

*Reprinted from Fortune by permission; © Time Inc. Year-end equity is referred to as invested capital by Fortune Magazine; it includes capital stocks, surplus and retained earnings.

how the debt ratios varied with differences in risk for four different industries, yet the returns on common equity were reasonably similar as follows:

| | | Finance | |
Industrials	Electric Utilities	Companies	Banks
14%	11%	15%	12%

These figures are only for a single year and they are results rather than what investors require. The return for the electric utilities is obviously lower than the return investors require, and reflects the problems utilities have had in obtaining adequate rate increases to overcome the effects of inflation. And banks' earnings have been poor. However the figures do suggest a similarity of return. In other words, for large well situated companies, debt ratio should vary with the risk of the business and equate out the risk to the common stockholders so that they should be willing to accept approximately the same return.

How large must a company be for this statement to hold true? That depends on the nature of the industry. Generally, sales of around $500,000,000 will begin to put most types of companies in the larger sized category for this purpose. Smaller companies do have more risk and a higher common cost rate, as do companies which have special risk factors.

We have merely suggested the general magnitude of the common cost rate; your financial vice president should be able to fine tune the figure for your company.

FOREIGN INVESTMENT

Foreign investment is a good example of higher risk. At times, when the world-wide economic picture looks favorable, the risks of foreign investment may not seem serious, but they will be felt in the long run.

If an investor had the opportunity of buying a stock of a company in this country or a stock of a similar company with its investment in a foreign country, there is little question that on the basis of an equal return he would quickly choose the investment in this country.

The obvious risks of foreign investment are:

1. Foreign exchange fluctuations
2. Problems of repatriating money.

And there are additional risks such as:

1. Different operating and management problems
2. Anti-Americanism
3. Possible confiscation

Considering these factors, the investor would want a substantially higher return, regardless of the country, and he would not even consider putting his money in some countries. For this reason, you should expect that investors will generally capitalize foreign earnings at a relatively low multiple.

Returns on foreign investment of U.S. companies have generally not been sufficiently above the returns in this country to adequately compensate for the added risk.[1]

You will have to have a higher return on your company's investment in foreign countries than the companies domiciled in those countries which get their capital internally. With a higher cost of capital you will have a competitive disadvantage.

These are capital investment problems which you should face up to when you invest abroad. And you should attempt to minimize the amount of capital committed abroad required to generate a certain amount of sales.

---

[1] Data on profitability of U.S. corporations from investment inside and outside the U.S. is published by Business International Corporation, One Dag Hammarskjold Plaza, N.Y. New York 10017.

MISLEADING FIGURES ON COMMON COSTS

Calculating the common cost rate is one of the most difficult parts of finance. If you are not an expert in the field, it is easy to be confused and come up with erroneous figures.

Sometimes, the dividend yield is referred to as the common cost. Not so, because all of the earnings belong to the common stockholders. Investors also receive market appreciation which comes from retained earnings.

You may feel that you can have the common cost for your company calculated from your company's historical figures. You may encounter so-called experts who will make the calculations for you. This cannot generally be done because, as we have said, common cost depends on the relationship of the market price of common stock to investor expectations and not what actually happened.

Another mistake is to assume that the common cost is the reciprocal of the price-earnings ratio, that is, the earnings-price ratio. For example, if a company earns $5.00 per share, and the stock sells for $100, the earnings-price ratio is 5%. This is definitely not the common cost. The only reason the stock is selling for $100 is because investors expect future earnings to increase.

This misconception regarding the earnings-price ratio sometimes leads management to believe that as their stock price goes up the common cost decreases. Generally this is not so. The reason stocks go up is because investors believe earnings are going up, not because investors will require a lower minimum return. Actually, the rate investors require for a particular risk in a common stock may only change gradually over a relatively long period of time.

CONCLUSION ON COMMON COST

In conclusion, the definition of common cost is:
THE MINIMUM RETURN REQUIRED TO INDUCE IN-VESTORS TO PROVIDE COMMON CAPITAL.

Or, THE RELATIONSHIP OF MARKET PRICE TO INVES-TORS' EXPECTATIONS WHEN THEY BUY A STOCK.

You should have a definite figure as to what is a minimum or break even rate for your company. That is the common cost. You should realize that if your company has a sound capital structure, and you earn below this figure on your stockholders' investment, you are in effect, losing money.

If your company is too heavily in debt, have your financial vice-president adjust the financial statements to conform to a proper ratio and then look at your return on common equity. To arrive at this adjusted figure, all that is required is to reduce debt in the balance sheet and add to common equity and correspondingly reduce interest charges and increase income taxes in the income statement.

And if your debt ratio is too high you might also have your financial vice-president show you what your earnings per share would look like with adequate common equity. This is a realistic approach and may prevent you from being misled by apparent favorable equity earnings due to excessive leverage.

A PROFIT GOAL

Having decided on what your capital costs are, the next step is to establish a profit goal for your company.

In the first place, the minimum rate we have been talking about would make the market price just equate out to the stockholders' investment on the balance sheet. This minimum return should be increased so as to permit a new offering of common at a price so that the net amount the company receives after paying financing costs will be at least equal to book value. In addition, the return should be higher so that in spite of the fluctuations of the market price of your company's stock, your company would have adequate access to the equity market without having to sell below book value.

Consideration also has to be given to the fact that some capital investments such as pollution investment do not provide any return. And some of your capital expenditures which show a forecast profit will turn out to be duds.

There is no mathematical way to decide on how high your profit goal should be to allow for the above factors. It is strictly a matter of judgment. And it will depend on what you think your ability is in satisfying consumers' needs in the face of competition. You must have a competitive edge to set a high goal or else you will price yourself out of the market.

We might say that if a large well-situated company with sound capitalization earned a return of about 13% on common equity, it would break even, 15% would be good and 17% excellent. Note how these figures compare with the returns earned by the Fortune 500 in Exhibit 2–2. You would have to set a profit goal above these respective rates to achieve these returns.

The utility industry faces a difficult problem in earning an adequate return in a period of inflation. By the time a rate increase is granted, expenses have already increased so as to erode away the allowed return. In other words, if a commission grants a rate increase based on what it considers to be a fair return, the company never gets to earn that return. Most regulatory commissions have not faced up to this problem. That is unfair to investors, and it makes raising the billions of dollars of capital the industry needs difficult. These companies have relatively high debt ratios as compared to industrial companies and must have adequate earnings coverage of interest to keep their bond ratings. And they must have adequate earnings to attract large amounts of common stock capital. Many experts testify that such companies need a return on common of around 15%. Regulatory commissions have allowed 13% and some as high as 14% and 15%.

In this chapter, we have been talking about the return on the book investment the stockholders made in your company. The present value of the assets may be much higher today because of inflation. As we have said, when an investor gave you his money with the idea that he expected you to earn a certain return, presumably he considered what the return should be in view of the prospects for inflation. However, it cannot be overlooked that the current value of a company's assets is a consideration in viewing the adequacy of the return that a company is making.

HOW THE PRECEDING DISCUSSION FITS INTO YOUR CAPITAL MANAGEMENT DECISIONS

After you have established rates for the various parts of long-term capital, that is, principally debt and common equity, the next step is to combine them so as to obtain an overall rate for long-term capital.

You will be interested in using the over-all rate for three purposes:

> As another way to measure the success of your company.
> For division performance standards
> For capital investment decisions.

Since the overall rate includes interest, you will have to be sure that your calculations give proper effect to corporate income taxes.

And there is one other very important factor to consider. The overall rate is determined on the liability side of the balance sheet on long-term capital. For division performance standards and capital investment decisions, you will be working with assets. The asset base may be different from the long-term capital base. It is necessary to convert the rate on long-term capital to a new rate which when applied to the asset base will produce the desired return on the long-term capital and the stockholders' investment.

The principles of cost-of-capital have to be applied in all calculations for division performance standards and project profitability analysis. The rate for a particular division or project has to be measured in terms of the overall cost of capital with the amount of debt that is appropriate for that particular risk.

Making these calculations is the job of your financial vice-president. However, we will describe the process briefly. If you wish further detail, Appendix I shows how the rates relate to balance sheet and income statement figures.

COMPANY PERFORMANCE MEASURE—TO INVESTOR RATE

The *To Investor Rate* is the starting point for the overall return on total long-term capital. This rate is used as another test of your company's performance in addtion to the return on stockholders' investment with a sound long-term capital.

For a moderate sized industrial company, a debt ratio of 27% would produce good quality debt given adequate earnings. If the interest rate on the debt is 8%, and the minimum return, or common cost, is 13%, the overall rate to investors on total capital would be 11.65% as shown following:

Long-term capital		Rate	Return
Debt	$ 27	8%	$ 2.16
Common	73	13%	9.49
Total	$100		$11.65

This overall rate is compared with the rate obtained by adding total interest payments on long-term debt to net income, and dividing by total long-term capital. If a company has too high a debt ratio, the overall rate is a better test of company's performance than return on the stockholders' investment. It eliminates that part of the effect of leverage due to interest. However, it does not eliminate the effect of the income tax reduction from too high debt. Since interest is deductable for income taxes, the greater the debt the higher the interest charges and the lower the income taxes.

DIVISION PERFORMANCE STANDARDS—PRE-TAX RATE

Generally a pre-tax rate is used for division performance standards. It should be 21.14% on the basis of the figures we have used assuming a 50% tax rate.

Long-term capital		Rate	Return
Debt	$27	8%	$ 2.16
Common	73	26%	18.98
Total	$100		$21.14

This rate must be adjusted to allow for the difference in the long-term capital and asset base on which division performance standards are measured.

Your company's divisions may have a wide range of profitability. Setting division performance standards is a complicated operation. The goal for each division must be established on a practical basis so that a division manager will feel that the goal is attainable. This may require a high goal for a favorably situated division and a lower goal for a less profitable division.

You must guard against setting standards which will induce managers to take actions which will be harmful to your company in the long run. For example, a very profitable division with a high goal should not necessarily turn down new projects with a return below the goal for its division just because the new project would pull down the division's average rate of return.

And a division manager should not be allowed to skimp on worthwhile long range capital expenditures just because they might hurt the manager's current return.

PROJECT PROFITABILITY—AFTER-TAX EQUIVALENT RATE

The analysis of the profitability of a capital investment is as complicated as division performance standards.

In the first place, your financial officer will undoubtedly calculate the profitability of a particular project in terms of discounted cash flow, but he may not discuss it with you in such terms. He might think that you would prefer a simpler method such as payback which shows the number of years it takes to get the capital back. Some of the calculations in discounting may be complex and must be done by an expert in order not to let errors creep in. However, the concept is elementary and should be understood by everyone on your management team. It is explained in Appendix II if you wish to refer to it.

The profitability of a project is calculated after taxes as though all of the capital were supplied by common stock. In other words, the taxes are not reduced by any interest payments. To the extent that a project can be financed appropriately with some debt, the income of the project is understated by the tax savings that the interest would produce.

To compensate for this understatement of income, the interest component in the hurdle rate is reduced by the tax savings that would be produced by the interest on the appropriate amount of debt. This is called the after-tax equivalent rate and in our example is 10.57% as follows:

Long-Term Capital		Rate	Return
Debt	$ 27	4%	$ 1.08
Common	73	13%	9.49
Total	$100		$10.57

The rate representing the risk of the project is developed on the basis of long-term capital and has to be adjusted to allow for the difference in the long-term capital base and the asset base, which is used in calculating the profitability of a project.

ACQUISITION PRICING AND SOME COMMENTS

AN ACQUISITION IS JUST ONE FORM OF CAPITAL IN-VESTMENT AND SHOULD BE ANALYZED THE SAME WAY.

In the 1960's, acquisition pricing was one of the major management blunders. As a consequence, some companies have large amounts of intangibles representing excessive prices paid for acquisitions on which an adequate return will never be earned.

In the first place, the decision regarding the price you pay for a company must be completely separated from how you finance it. In the 1960's, acquisition decisions were made mostly on the basis of how they were financed and on the effect on current earnings per share, a totally incorrect basis. Unfortunately, today many companies don't seem to have learned from past mistakes and are paying ridiculous prices for acquisitions. The stockholders of the acquiring company would undoubtedly be better off if the funds used for an acquisition were given to them in the form of extra dividends or through repurchase of their common stock. Then they could use "their money" to purchase stocks of other companies in the market at much lower prices. And they would have a better chance of earning a fair return than an acquiring company might earn on an excessive purchase price. In Appendix III is a relatively simple way to look at the return on investment in an acquisition.

We might comment that in establishing your acquisition program you should be sensitive about how investors may view your company. Diversification of the wrong kind may kill investors interest. For example, suppose an insurance company is merged with a manufacturing company or visa versa, analysts interested in insurance companies may lose interest, and analysts interested in manufacturing companies may do likewise. A senior investment officer of an insurance company put it this way: *I want to know the direction your company is heading. Diversification in all different directions kills my interest.*

This is, of course, a very general statement, but your financial officer should have his ear to the ground and be able to help you in this decision.

Some companies are now acquiring the entire common stocks of companies as so-called investments. There is no way that an acquiring company can avoid, at least, the prospect of having to manage the company once it owns the entire stock. In order to avoid managing the company, it would have to have liquidity so that it could sell its "investment" if the outlook dimmed—and liquidity it does not have. That type of investment management is performed in our economic system by investment companies which do have liquidity. Furthermore, if the management of an acquiring company does not manage the company it acquires, what is the management doing for their salaries?

It is sad to watch our free enterprise system abused so badly by some managements making unsound acquisition decisions and seeing directors sit idly by. They are certainly not thinking of the good of their stockholders.

CONCLUSION

In conclusion: AN UNDERSTANDING OF THE CONCEPT OF THE COST OF COMMON EQUITY AND HOW CAPITAL STRUCTURE SHOULD VARY WITH RISK ARE ABSOLUTELY BASIC TO FINANCIAL PLANNING AND HANDLING ALL ASPECTS OF CAPITAL MANAGEMENT.

Chapter 3

HOW MUCH EARNINGS TO PAY OUT IN DIVIDENDS?

Cash dividends are one of the few items in the budget almost entirely variable at your discretion.

Dividends are supposedly the prerogative of the directors. What generally happens is that the management makes a recommendation and the directors approve it. In any event, you and your directors should be well versed in dividend policy because of its importance.

DIVIDEND IMPORTANCE

Dividends are a major part of financial planning for four reasons:

1. They are a part of stockholders' return.
2. They may affect the price of a stock. If they do, then they affect:
   a. Market appreciation, the other part of the stockholders' return.
   b. The price the company receives when it sells new stock.

75

3. They may affect a company's ability to sell stock.
4. They reduce the amount of retained earnings. Consequently they affect:
   a. The amount of financing required.
   b. The percent of debt to total long-term capital.
   c. The equity base on which to increase earnings per share.

VARIOUS APPROACHES

There are various approaches to dividend policy such as:

1. Pay what other companies in your industry pay.
2. Let your stockholders share in good earnings.
3. Consider your needs for cash and earned surplus, and then decide what to pay your stockholders. This is known as the residual approach.
4. Pay no dividends. Retain all of your earnings on the assumption that your stockholders will be better off with the company putting the earnings to work in the business.

We will comment on these approaches and show why we believe that they do not provide the correct answer.

WHICH COMES FIRST, STOCKHOLDERS' DESIRE FOR DIVIDENDS OR YOUR COMPANY'S NEED FOR CASH?

The first question that has to be answered is whether dividends or a company's need for funds take priority. At this point, we are not suggesting a company should or should not pay a dividend. We are merely raising the question as to whether consideration of dividend policy comes ahead of cash needs. It is essential that you come to grips with this question at the start, because your subsequent reasoning will be quite different depending on your answer.

A company may be in one of three different positions with regard to the need for funds:

1. A financially weak company which cannot raise outside capital may need funds for such basic purposes as:

   Maturing debt.

   Maintenance of a minimum working capital position.

   Capital investment in order to save its existing investment.

   Sacrificing dividends for a financially weak company may hurt stockholders through loss of cash dividends and the adverse market action of the stock. However, in such a situation a company may have no alternative.

2. A company may be sufficiently strong to meet basic demands for cash, but it may be unable to raise outside capital for expansion. In such a situation, a question arises as to whether a company should ignore stockholders' wishes for dividends and conserve cash for such expansion. If the expansion would improve the position of the stockholders so as to more than offset any harm from limiting cash dividend payments, such a policy would be appropriate. The return on investment would have to be very attractive in order to justify such action.

   For a commerical bank the need for equity may be the inhibiting factor rather than the need for funds.

3. Finally, a company may be in a satisfactory financial position so as to be able to raise outside capital.

   In this situation, dividend policy comes first because of three reasons mentioned above about the importance of dividends: they are a part of stockholders' income, they may affect the price of the stock and they may affect a company's ability to sell stock.

To summarize: IF A COMPANY IS WEAK FINANCIALLY, DIVIDENDS MAY HAVE TO BE SACRIFICED REGARDLESS

OF THE CONSEQUENCES. IF A COMPANY IS STRONG FI-
NANCIALLY, DIVIDEND POLICY SHOULD COME FIRST
AND, IF NECESSARY, THE NEED FOR FUNDS OR COM-
MON SHOULD BE SATISFIED BY FINANCING.

GROWTH RATE IN EARNINGS PER SHARE FROM PLOWBACK

In order to establish a dividend policy, it is necessary to understand the effect of dividing net income between dividends and
retained earnings.

Retention of earnings builds up the stockholders' capital and is
the principal way earnings per share grow. This is illustrated in
three parts in Exhibit 3–1 which we will now explain.

Part I is a simple example. It shows the common book value per
share at the beginning of year 1 to be $100. The return is 10% so
earnings per share are $10. The dividend payout ratio is 50% so the
dividend is $5 and retained earnings are $5. The $5 retained is added
to the book value per share so that the book value at the beginning of
year 2 is $105. The company continues to earn 10% so earnings per
share in year 2 increases to $10.50. The dividend payout ratio stays
the same at 50% so the dividend is now $5.25 and retained earnings
$5.25.

The increases are due to the increase in investment from retaining 50% of the earnings and putting them to work at the same 10%
rate as on the original investment. In other words, the $5 retained in
the first year is reinvested at 10% to produce $0.50 more earnings
per share, resulting in a 5% increase.

As long as the return on the common book value and dividend
payout ratio stay the same, the growth rates will be constant. They
can be obtained from the formula shown in Part II. It states that the
growth rate is a result of multiplying the percent earned times the
percent of earnings retained. The percent of earnings retained is
100% less the percent paid out. Of course a change in earnings on

Exhibit 3-1

GROWTH RATE IN EARNINGS PER SHARE FROM PLOWBACK

Part I

Illustration

Constant Rate of Return on Beginning Book Value, Dividend Payout Ratio and Price-Earnings Ratio

Column	1	2	3	4	5	6	7	8
Year	Beginning[1] Common Stock Book Value per Share	Return on Beginning[1] Book Value	Earnings per Share Common Stock	Dividend Payout Ratio	Dividends per Share	Retained Earnings per Share	Price-Earnings Ratio	Market Price per Share
1	$100.00	10%	$10.00	50%	$5.00	$5.00	10	$100.00
2	105.00	10	10.50	50	5.25	5.25	10	105.00
3	110.25	10	11.025	50	5.5125	5.5125	10	110.25
Growth Rate	5%		5%		5%	5%		5%

79

Part II

Formula
(Figures from Part I)

% Earned on Beginning[1] Book Value	×	% of Earnings Retained	=	Growth Rate in Book Value per Share, Earnings per Share and Dividends per Share.
"	×	100% minus % of Earnings Paid Out	=	"
10%	×	50%(50% paid out)	=	5%

Part III

Growth Rates in Earnings per Share from Plowback
for Various Rates of Return and Payouts

% Earned on Beginning[1] Book Value	×	% of Earnings Retained	=	Growth Rate
10%	×	50%(50% paid out)	=	5.0%
13	×	58%(42% paid out)	=	7.5
15	×	63%(37% paid out)	=	9.5
17	×	68%(32% paid out)	=	11.6

[1]The return on common book value is based on beginning book value because it is used to calculate the growth rate in earnings per share from plowback. The retained earnings come out of earnings during the year and are added to next year's beginning book value. Consequently, the compounding effect of plowback takes place with beginning book value as the base.

---

past investment will affect earnings per share, but this is aside from the effect of the earnings retained or, in other words, plowed back into the company.

To further illustrate the formula, it is applied to various rates of return and payouts in Part III.

To the extent that a company retains earnings, investors do not get dividends. But, as we have illustrated, the retained earnings build up earnings per share which in turn results in market appreciation equal to the growth rate in earnings per share if the price-earnings ratio remains constant. This as shown in Part I, columns 7 and 8.

ARGUMENTS AGAINST PAYING DIVIDENDS

The arguments used against paying dividends are as follows:

1. The company can obtain common equity without paying any financing costs.
2. If investors need some cash they can sell some of their holdings.
3. The tax rate is higher on dividend income than on capital gains.
4. The company may be able to reinvest the retained earnings at a higher rate than investors could invest money they receive from dividends. And brokerage fees have to be paid by investors if they reinvest.
5. Those who contend that a company should not pay dividends will argue that dividends have no effect on price.

REASONS WHY A COMPANY SHOULD CONSIDER PAYING DIVIDENDS

The following ideas argue in favor of dividends:

1. In the first place, the suggestion that a company should not pay dividends because retained earnings build up equity and avoid the sale of stock should not carry much weight.

There is no loss to the stockholders as far as the money paid out is concerned because it goes to them, the owners. All that is lost is financing costs to raise new funds through the sale of common.

2. Many investors do not like to treat dividends and market appreciation as interchangeable. They want to keep their investment and not have to sell part in order to get income. As a practical matter, if stockholders sell a small amount of their investment to obtain cash, the brokerage expense will be high.

3. Investors vary widely as to their tax advantage of capital gains vs dividend income. And there is a wide variation in institutional investors' interest in the tax treatment of capital gains vs dividend income. Corporations recieve an 85% dividend tax credit. Mutual insurance companies pay a lower corporate tax rate. Charitable institutions are tax exempt.

4. Other things being equal, dividends are more valuable to stockholders than prospects of an equal amount of market appreciation because there is risk in market appreciation. Dividends are a bird in the hand while market appreciation depends on the company's ability to put the capital to work at an adequate return and the market to translate the increase in earnings into market appreciation.

   This is particularly important for fund managers in view of the sour results that they have produced in the past. Dividends give assurance of certain income.

5. Some investors won't buy stocks that don't pay dividends.

6. Some investors cannot legally buy common stocks unless they have a dividend record. For example, common stocks to be eligible for investment by New York savings banks must, among other things, have paid cash dividends on their common stocks in each year for a period of ten years next preceding the date of investment.

7. Some investors cannot consider income from dividends and market appreciation as interchangeable. In trust funds, laws distinguish between dividends and market

appreciation which respectively accrue to the life beneficiary and the remainder man. The trustee will wish to
choose investments which will be fair to both and would be
interested in stocks paying dividends in order to give some
return to the life beneficiary.

8. Some institutional investors cannot, for accounting or legal
reasons, treat dividends and market appreciation as interchangeable.

9. Dividends may put a floor on the market price of a stock
when earnings are adverse and the yield becomes significant. When a stock is selling at a high price-earnings ratio
and a low yield this advantage of a dividend may seem
quite remote. But if a company runs into trouble so that
the market price of the stock sinks, a high yield tends to
prevent stockholders from selling and may attract investors who feel that the dividend gives them a satisfactory
return as well as protection against further decline.

10. Dividends may add stability to the market price of a stock
because dividends should fluctuate less than earnings.

11. If dividend policy affects the market price, then stockholders benefit when the company sells new stock because
of the better price the company receives. This improves
existing stockholders' book value. Earnings per share increase if new stock is sold above book value and the company is able to earn at least the same return on the new
book value as on the existing. This we will explain subsequently.

12. Your investment banker may stress the importance of
dividends when you sell new stock.

Thus, there is a wide range of interest in dividends on the part of
both individual and institutional investors. It does make a difference
to some investors whether earnings are paid out or retained for
certain types of companies.

In view of the interest of some investors in dividends, how do you
make a decision regarding an appropriate policy for your company?

CORRELATION BETWEEN PRICE-EARNINGS RATIO AND
DIVIDEND PAYOUT RATIO

In order to determine the most appropriate dividend policy for a company, it would be ideal if a large sample could be obtained of exactly similar companies but with different dividend payout policies. Then a correlation table could be developed which would show the payout ratio which would produce the highest price-earnings ratio. This generally cannot be done for two reasons.

1. It is difficult to obtain a broad sample of companies which are sufficiently similar except for dividend policy so that the effect of dividend policy alone can be determined. So many other factors affect the price-earnings ratio such as the type of business, the outlook for earnings, etc.
2. It is future earnings as expected by investors which affect the common stock market price and not current earnings. Therefore, in developing such a correlation table, the relationship of market price to future earnings expected by investors should be used rather than a price-earnings ratio based on current earnings. As a practical matter, it would be impossible to obtain a representative cross section of earnings expected by investors for this purpose.

There are a few exceptions to the above comments. For example in the electric utility industry, in which there is relative uniformity, it has been possible at times to show a strong correlation between dividends as a percent of book value and market price related to book value. But generally you cannot use this type of statistical analysis to determine dividend policy.

WHAT OTHER SIMILAR COMPANIES HAVE DONE

You will naturally want to consider the policies of other similar companies in your industry. But you cannot use them to determine a policy for your company because their policies may not be correct.

When you do study the policies followed by other companies, you have to keep in mind that a high or low payout ratio for a company in any one year may not be indicative of a company's policy. It may be the result of unusually low or high earnings. To get a clue as to a company's payout policy, the results should be studied over at least a five-year period as well as all the circumstances surrounding the company, such as the level of the company's earnings, the company's financial strength, availability of profitable investment projects, etc.

In studying what other companies have done, it may be interesting to observe the immediate effect on the market price of a stock when dividends were changed. However, the immediate market effect of a change may not be discernible for three reasons:

1. The market may have anticipated the change so that at the time the change is made the market action may already have been spent.
2. A dividend change may cause market action due to investors interpreting the change as an indication of a favorable outlook for the company's earnings. Investors are aware that the directors must consider a company's prospects when deciding on dividend policy.
3. Other factors may affect the stock price at the time of the increase and negate or overshadow the effect of the dividend change.

Thus far we have given you necessary background material on dividend policy; now we are ready to suggest an approach to determine a policy for your company.

TWO QUESTIONS—AMOUNT AND TYPE

There are two major questions that have to be determined:

1. The amount.
2. The type of payment—regular, variable, extra.

The type and amount are to a degree interdependent; type will have an effect on amount.

We will first consider the amount of the payment.

THE GOAL—ATTRACT GREATEST NUMBER OF STOCKHOLDERS

In order to determine a dividend policy for your company, the goal should be to establish a policy which will appeal to the greatest number of stockholders over the long run. By enhancing the demand for your stock, you should improve the market price.

Occasionally, you may hear the management of a company say that dividend policy should be established which will attract the type of investors the company wants.

This is putting the cart before the horse. Such a policy would not necessarily result in the greatest benefit to stockholders in the long run because it might reduce the long range total demand for the stock.

The type of company itself, regardless of the dividend policy, will have much to do with the type of investors which it attracts. A new speculative company will tend to attract investors who are willing to take a large risk and want capital gains exclusively. Such investors tend to be in the high income tax bracket. Dividends would be an annoyance to them.

A strong, well-established company with a high return on common can do more for stockholders by retaining a high percentage of earnings. It can probably reinvest the money at a better rate than its stockholders could do if earnings were paid out in dividends. Furthermore, retention of a large part of the earnings will result in a fast growth in earnings per share from the effect of plowback. This should produce a high price-earnings ratio which will add to market appreciation. Such a company will tend to attract investors who want some dividends but have most interest in market appreciation. This calls for a low payout.

You may feel that such a company should not pay any dividends. However, as we have said, dividends are a bird in the hand. Here is the opinion of one man who spent a long career in investment management. T. Rowe Price made the following comment[1] about dividends for growth stocks: "A non-dividend growth stock is not worth as high a price-earnings ratio as a dividend-payer, assuming quality is the same."

A stable type of company which does not have an opportunity to invest its capital at a high rate of return will tend to attract investors who are more interested in income from dividends. A higher payout fits such a company best.

In other words, you cannot change the nature of your company with dividend policy. Therefore, in order to achieve the goals we have suggested A DIVIDEND POLICY SHOULD BE ESTAB-LISHED WHICH WILL ENHANCE AND STRENGTHEN IN-VESTORS' NATURAL INTEREST IN YOUR COMPANY IN THE LONG RUN.

SELECTION OF DIVIDEND PAYOUT PERCENTAGE BY PROCESS OF ELIMINATION THROUGH JUDGMENT

Since a statistical approach cannot generally be used to determine dividend policy, it is necessary to rely on judgment and establish a policy which will enhance and strengthen the natural interest of investors in your company.

There are basically five dividend polices in terms of percent payout. They are given in Exhibit 3–2 with comments indicating the types of companies which they might fit. The percentages for each policy are merely indications of appropriate percentages. Actually, each policy is a percentage band. Dividend policy cannot be deter-mined with a great degree of precision and need not be. All that is

---

[1]"Market Place. T. Rowe Price Views Growth Stocks." © 1977 by the New York Times Company. Reprinted by permission.

necessary is to establish a payout policy within reasonable limits. The five policies can be summarized as follows:

1. 0%
   For a company which attracts investors who are seeking capital gains.
2. Nominal—5% to 10%
   To build a dividend record prior to paying a significant dividend.
3. Low—around ⅓
   For a company which can reinvest earnings at a high rate of return.
4. Average—40% to 50%
   For a typical industrial company with a moderate return on capital.
5. High—65% to 70%
   For a stable type of company which has a moderate return and to which investors look for large dividends.

Exhibit 3–2

Five Types of Dividend Payout Ratios

1. *0%*

   For a company with speculative characteristics which will only attract investors who are seeking capital gains.

2. *Nominal—5% to 10%*

   For a company in a transition period from the type with no cash dividend to a more stable type of company prior to paying a significant dividend.

   Such a nominal dividend will not mean much to stockholders, and it will have little effect on market price. However, the purpose is to build a dividend record to satisfy investors in the future who are attracted to a type of company which has a sustained dividend record.

3. *Low—around ⅓*

For a company with a sound capital structure which gener-
ates a good return such as 15% or more.

It is unlikely that the company's stockholders could reinvest
the dividends at as high a rate. Furthermore, such a company can do more for investors with a low payout because
the high growth rate in earnings per share will produce a
high price-earnings ratio. In order for this to happen, the
company must have new capital investment opportunities
which will provide a high return.

For a company with a high return on capital, a high growth
rate and a high price-earnings ratio the yield to the investor
based on market price will be relatively small. However, it
may attract investors who would not buy the stock if it paid
no dividends. A steady upward dividend pattern gives confidence to investors. If the company runs into trouble, the
dividend will eventually act as a stabilizing influence as the
market price declines. Furthermore, while the yield may
be low based on the current dividend related to market
price, investors may look ahead to dividend increases and
anticipate a satisfactory yield on their original investment.

A company with a high return on common equity due to
excessive leverage should have a low payout for another
reason: the earnings are vulnerable to decline.

4. *Average—40% to 50%*

For a typical large industrial company earning approximately 13% on the beginning common book value.

Because of the variability of earnings of a typical industrial
company, a higher payout might make the dividend vulnerable to being cut.

5. *High—65% to 70%*

For a stable type of company like a large utility or a large
money center bank which cannot earn a high return on its
common book value but does have stability of earnings.

It can offer a generous dividend without fear of cutting it.
This will appeal to the broad group of investors who want a
high yield.

PROBLEMS IN ESTABLISHING A DIVIDEND POLICY

In establishing a dividend policy, you have to start with the idea of
paying out a percent of earnings. However, this results in a problem.

Let's assume that your company is a moderate earner in the
neighborhood of 13% on beginning common book value and you
decide that a payout of 42% will enhance and strengthen the natural
interest of investors in your company.

Next year earnings improve and the return goes to 15%. Now
what do you do, payout 42%? No, because this would result in too
precipitous an increase. Furthermore, with a higher earning rate
you can justify a lower payout. Therefore, you have to determine
another payout policy. There is a solution to this problem which also
makes it easy to lay out a policy.

DIVIDEND RELATED TO BOOK VALUE,
A HELPFUL APPROACH

Having estabslished a payout policy with a certain rate of return,
then calculate the dividend as a percent of beginning book value.
For example, with a 13% return and a 42% payout, the dividend will
be 5.5% of book value. If the dividend is kept at this percent of book
value, the dividend will increase as the book value increases from
retained earnings. And what is more important, the percent payout
will vary correctly as the rate of return varies. For example, if the
dividend is kept at 5.5% on beginning book value and the return

increases to 15%, the payout will drop to 37%, and if the return increases to 17%, the payout will drop to 32%. Thus, as the return goes up the percent payment decreases, as it should, and vise versa.

Furthermore, it is logical to relate dividends to book value because earnings, out of which dividends are paid, are related to book value to measure how well a company is doing. And dividends as a percent of book value tells you immediately how much you have to earn on the common book value to just cover the dividend.

Dividends as a percent of book value is probably a better indicator of a company's policy because it eliminates the effect of good and bad earnings on the measurement of dividends.

Exhibit 3–3 shows how the payout varies as the return changes for various rates of dividends as a percent of book value. We have included dividends as a percent of book value at 5.0% and 6% which today might be a range for a typical industrial company, and 8.5% which is even too low currently for an electric utility.

In other words, you should consider what is a sustainable rate of return on your common equity. Then by process of elimination pick one of the five policies which is most likely to enhance and strengthen the natural interest of investors in your company in the long run. As a final step, determine what that dividend would represent as a percent of common book value and use that percentage to determine future dividend policy regardless of the rate of return. As the return varies above and below the sustainable rate of return, the payout will decrease and increase as it should. Your long range growth rate in dividends will be your sustainable rate of return times the percent of earnings retained.

DIVIDEND DATA FOR THREE INDUSTRIES

Now that we have suggested an approach to determine the amount a company should pay, we will look at dividend payments for three quite different industries: manufacturing companies, electric utilities and commercial banks. This is shown in Exhibit 3–4.

Exhibit 3–3

**Dividend Policies for
Certain Industrial and Electric Utility Companies**

DIVIDENDS AS A PERCENT OF BEGINNING COMMON BOOK VALUE	Industrial 5%		Electric Utility 8.5%	
Return on Beginning Common Book Value	*Dividend Payout Ratio*	*Growth Rate from Plowback*	*Dividend Payout Ratio*	*Growth Rate from Plowback*
13%	38%	8%	65%	4.5%
15	33	10	57	6.5
17	29	12		
20	25	15		

DIVIDENDS AS A PERCENT OF BEGINNING COMMON BOOK VALUE	6%	
Return on Beginning Common Book Value	*Dividend Payout Ratio*	*Growth Rate from Plowback*
13%	46%	7%
15	40	9
17	35	11
20	30	14

Exhibit 3–4

Comparative Dividend Ratios for Industrial Companies, Electric Utilities and Banks

Industrial Companies

Column	I	II	III	IV	V	VI	VII	VIII	IX
	ALL MANUFACTURING COMPANIES			STANDARD & POOR'S 400 INDUSTRIALS					
	Return on Average Equity	Dividend Payout Ratio	Dividends as a % of Average Book Value	Return on Average Equity	Dividend Payout Ratio	Dividends as a % of Average Book Value	Dividend Yield	Market Price Divided by Book Value	Price-Earnings Ratio
Line									
1 1977	14.3%	38%	5.4%	14.6%	43%	6.3%	4.5%	138%	9.5x
2 1976	14.1	35	5.0	14.5	40	5.7	3.8	152	10.5
3 5-year Average 1973–1977	13.7	38	5.0	14.2	41	5.8	3.9	151	10.7
4 5-year Average 1968–1972	10.7	47	5.0	11.6	53	6.1	3.0	203	17.4

Column		I	II	III	IV	V	VI	VII	VIII	IX
Line		Return on Average Equity	Dividend Payout Ratio	Dividends as a % of Average Book Value	Return on Average Equity	Dividend Payout Ratio	Dividends as a % of Average Book Value	Dividend Yield	Market Price Divided by Book Value	Price-Earnings Ratio

Electric Utilities

		PRIVATE ELECTRIC UTILITY INDUSTRY			MOODY'S 24 ELECTRIC UTILITIES					
5	1977	11.4%	68%	7.8%	11.4%	62%	7.1%	8.2%	87%	7.6x
6	1976	11.5	67	7.7	10.7	64	6.8	8.6	79	7.4
7	5-year Average 1973–1977	11.2	67	7.6	10.7	64	6.9	8.7	80	7.5
8	5-year Average 1968–1972	11.9	67	8.0	11.4	66	7.5	5.4	141	12.4

Commercial Banks

		ALL INSURED U.S. BANKS			SIX MAJOR NEW YORK CITY BANKS					
9	1977	11.7%	37%	4.4%	10.5%	45%	4.7%	5.8%	81%	7.7x
10	1976	11.4	39	4.4	10.6	45	4.8	5.6	86	8.1
11	5-year Average 1973–1977	12.0	39	4.7	11.9	44	5.2	5.2	102	8.6
12	5-year Average 1968–1972	11.9	42	5.0	11.4	54	6.0	4.0	146	13.6

94

Columns I, II, and III provide data on dividend payments for all companies in these three industries.

The other columns show data on stock indexes for these three industries with market price data.

Briefly, the figures indicate the following:

Manufacturing Companies

While cash payments generally increased, the payout ratio fell because earnings increased faster than dividends.

Dividends as a percent of book value decreased until recently when companies responded to investors' expressed interest.

Electric Utilities Companies

Their payout ratio has been relatively constant, but, related to book value, dividends tended to fall until recently. Now that figure is rising back to the old level of over 8%. Electric utility companies have had to sell large amounts of common stock. In order to do so at prices close to book value, managements have recognized that the market required a yield of around 9%.

Commercial Banks

They have been poor earners like the electric utilities, but unlike the electric utilities, they have let their dividends drift off badly. This is shown by the steady decline in relationship to book value.

Banks have not even been paying a dividend related to book value which is equivalent to the yield on the market price. Thus, their low dividends have combined with poor earnings as well as inadequate common equity to depress bank stocks below book value. Today, they face a dilemma: if they keep their dividends down to build up equity with retained earnings, their stocks will sell below book value so they don't want to sell stock. Some banks might consider higher dividends to get their stocks up and then sell common to build up equity.

With regard to the skimpy amount of equity of many banks, we suggest that banks might hesitate to make a loan to a finance company which had as small an equity in relation to risk assets.

TYPE OF DIVIDEND AND PATTERN

Now we turn to the type of dividend and the importance of pattern.

Past dividends are over the dam when investors buy a stock. Investors are concerned with what they may get in the future. However past dividends are important to the extent that they give a clue about the future. For this reason, the past pattern is very important.

A policy of paying out the same percentage of earnings each year would result in irregular dividends. This would not help to stablize the market price of a company's stock; predictions about dividends would have as much uncertainty as predictions about earnings.

A regular fixed dividend with no increase is a reflection of the company's inability to earn an adequate return on the retained earnings. The retained portion of the earnings remains in the company and increases the stockholders' equity. A company should earn on the added investment which should result in increased earnings per share and an increase in dividends.

If we combine regularity, or predictability, with an increasing dividend, then the result is the most desirable type: regular increasing regularly. By increasing regularly, we mean regular percentage increases and not regular amounts. If the earnings showed a regular percentage increase, the payout would decrease if the dividend was increased a constant dollar amount.

In order for a pattern to be effective, it must be believed by investors. They cannot use a past pattern for projecting into the future unless it is plausible. You should keep this in mind when establishing a dividend program. If the prospects for your company's earnings don't justify an increase, hold the dividend level. However, just because earnings are not good in one year, do not hesitate to increase the dividend if you are sure the outlook is favorable.

If what we have said above holds water, then an extra dividend will not help to achieve your goal. The market price of the company's stock will not be permanently affected to any material extent by an extra. It can be useful when a company has unusually good earnings and cannot invest retained earnings at an adequate return.

STOCK DIVIDENDS

We will comment only briefly on the subject of stock dividends, which are dividends paid in shares of stock. They cut up your stock into more pieces with each piece having a lower value, but the value of the total number of pieces being the same as before.

To distinguish a stock dividend from a stock split, the New York Stock Exchange has an arbitrary rule that the issuance of 24% of stock or less is a stock dividend and 25% or more is a stock split.

A few companies seem to think that stock dividends do something for their stockholders. In order to try to convince an executive who likes them that they are a waste of time often requires a long explanation. Since very few companies are interested in them, we will merely make the following remark. They may be said to be as useless as the way a little girl tried to get a longer blanket; she cut one end off and sewed it on the other end.

The primary reason for your being versed in the subject is because you may have to answer questions at your stockholders' annual meeting, in letters from your stockholders who are not knowledgeable in finance, etc. There is literature available for your financial vice-president to furnish you if the occassion arises.

CUTTING DIVIDENDS

If dividends have the purpose we have suggested, then cutting dividends is bound to have adverse effects.

1. Investors suffer an immediate cash loss which makes them place a lower evaluation on the stock as far as dividend income is concerned.
2. Investors may become fearful of what a dividend cut may signal. They may worry about what is wrong with the outlook for the company which made it necessary for management to cut the dividend.
3. It hurts the historical dividend pattern which investors study. They may ask if the company cut dividends in the past, will this happen again in the future? That will tend to undermine rather than build their faith.

Therefore, a company which has satisfactory financial strength should try hard not to cut a dividend. It should not fear a temporary high payout percentage as earnings decrease, and it should not hesitate to dip into earned surplus. It should not hesitate to borrow money to pay dividends if it is strong financially. In fact, we might make the bold statement that a company should not cut its dividend unless it is about to go down the drain. And it might as well go down the drain with its flag flying. This statement may be a little on the strong side, but we like to use it to emphasize the importance of not cutting a dividend.

COMPANY WITH EXCESS CASH

Warning! If you do not expect to earn at least your cost of capital on new projects, you have no justification for retaining earnings on the grounds that the company needs money for expansion.

While a strong liquid position is good, a company should not hold huge amounts of cash just on the vague assumption that some-time, somehow, it might be handy to have. On the other hand, a company which is expanding should not hesitate to keep cash available for any reasonable prospect for expansion.

A company with excess cash has various possibilities:

1. If the rate on its senior securities is high and they can be retired on reasonable terms, excess cash can be used for this purpose.

2. It can pay an extra dividend at the end of the year in order to distribute cash. Or it can have a high regular dividend payout policy if the company expects to generate extra cash continuously. You will observe some companies which have a high return on common book value with a relatively high payout policy for this reason.

3. It can repurchase its stock in the market for other than such routine corporate purposes as stock options, etc.

    Repurchase of stock should not be used to increase earnings per share and the price of the stock; this is a short range manipulative operation which will be self-defeating in the long run.

    Purchase of stock is an admission of your company's inability to use capital to generate earnings, and it has a negative connotation for the long-run outlook for the stock. However it may be the right thing to do if you have cash for which you see no possible need, your debt ratio is in line, and the stock can be obtained at an appropriate price.

    And purchase of your stock, if the price is appropriate, is far better than paying some fool price for an acquisition.

DIVIDEND REINVESTMENT

A dividend reinvestment plan assists stockholders in using their dividends to purchase additional shares of a company's outstanding stock. Presumably, if investors purchase a stock paying a dividend they want the income. As a matter of fact, the percentage of stockholders using dividend reinvestment plans offered by most companies is relatively small. If many stockholders used such a plan it would be an indication that the stockholders would prefer the company pay less dividends.

It should be noted that if a company pays the brokerage cost to purchase outstanding stock, the company is providing a special benefit to a small part of their stockholders, and the other stockholders might have a right to complain.

Some utility companies have used dividend reinvestment plans to assist in raising new capital because of their need for continuous large amounts of new capital. They issue new stock. The stockholders avoid the brokerage cost that would be incurred if they purchased stock and the company gets new common without having to pay an underwriting fee. In this special situation dividend reinvestment plans have been helpful.

In evaluating the advisability of a dividend reinvestment plan, a company should consider whether it will have any adverse effect on the market price of its stock. To the extent that stockholders get stock through dividend reinvestment rather than by purchasing shares in the market, the demand for the stock in the market is reduced. This may affect the market price.

DATES OF PAYMENTS

For a company which pays a significant dividend, quarterly payments are most desirable for investors. One increase a year is preferable to two increases because it is possible to build a better pattern over a period of years and it is less confusing to investors. Furthermore, in order to build investor confidence, it may be preferable to increase the dividend in the same quarter each year. A utility company may have difficulty in following this latter policy because it may not wish to increase the dividend just before it files for a rate increase.

INFORMATION ABOUT DIVIDEND POLICY

Dividends are dear to stockholders' hearts. Yet managements tend to be secretive about dividend policy. This may be due to the fact that managements do not have a structured dividend policy. Or it may be due to the fact that it is a difficult policy to explain. However, in the annual report it may be feasible to discuss the factors which affected the decision regarding a dividend change and the relationship between the payments and earnings. Following is an explanation used by one company. We do not necessarily agree with some of the reasoning used, but it does help investors understand the company's policy.

> In keeping with our policy of increasing the common stock dividend when justified by earnings, in May this year, your directors increased the dividend for the sixth consecutive year, this time to an annual rate of $2.25 from $1.75. Total dividends paid as a percentage of earnings were 27.3%. We have pursued a policy of lowering the ratio of dividends paid to earnings, both to improve the quality of the dividend and to provide internally generated funds for your company's substantial growth. It is management's present view, subject to the continuing approval of the board of directors, that this ratio should fluctuate about the 30% mark.

SUMMARY—ESTABLISHING A DIVIDEND POLICY

In order to establish a dividend policy for your company, take the following steps:

1. CONSIDER WHAT YOUR COMPANY HAS TO OFFER STOCKHOLDERS AND WHAT TYPE OF STOCK- HOLDERS MIGHT NATURALLY BE ATTRACTED TO YOUR COMPANY REGARDLESS OF DIVIDEND PAYMENTS.

   This includes an assessment of the average rate of return which your company can earn on your common stock book value, and whether you can reinvest the retained earnings at an appropriate rate.

2. BY PROCESS OF ELIMINATION, DECIDE WHICH OF THE FIVE PAYOUT POLICIES DISCUSSED WOULD MOST NEARLY FIT YOUR COMPANY IN VIEW OF ITS NATURE, EARNING ABILITY, AND THE TYPE OF STOCKHOLDERS WHO WOULD NATURALLY BE ATTRACTED TO IT.

3. APPLY THE PAYOUT RATIO TO YOUR AVERAGE RATE OF RETURN ON COMMON BOOK VALUE AND THEN RELATE THE DIVIDEND PAYMENT TO THE BOOK VALUE.

   By keeping approximately the same dividend rate as per- cent of book value, the payout ratio will change correctly as the return on common book value changes.

Dividend pattern is very important to show a record to investors. After a policy has been established with the above approach, then payments should be smoothed out so that they will produce an attractive record. Never make a decision on one dividend increase without considering how it may fit in with past and future moves.

Don't mislead investors by dividend payments which can't be justified. However, don't cut a dividend unless you are in deep trouble.

As a matter of fact, dividend policy is your best investor relations tool. You put your money where your mouth is. It is contradictory to complain that your price-earnings ratio is too low and yet be fearful of paying a satisfactory dividend because you feel that the outlook for your company is too risky.

A change in the capital gains tax may have some effect on dividend policy depending on its size and on how investors react. However, you should not make a quick change in dividend policy and the general approach suggested above can still be used to arrive at an appropriate policy for your company.

Chapter 4

HOW THE THREE RATIOS CIRCUMSCRIBE YOUR COMPANY'S FUTURE AND WHAT ELSE FOLLOWS

If you have established goals for the three financial ratios with your financial vice-president, you should be able to see how they circumscribe where your company can go if it does not sell common stock.

Of course, there are many factors which affect a company's progress. And the composition of a company's business and risk may change which will require a change in goals. However, we will use a simple example to illustrate how the three ratios affect your company's future balance sheet and income statement.

Suppose that yours is a successful industrial company. We will assume that your sales are $200,000,000 and long-term capital is $100,000,000. The figures we will refer to are shown in Exhibit 4–1.

You have established goals as follows:

Long-term debt as percent of total long-term capital	27%
Return on beginning common equity	15%
Dividend payout ratio	37%

The return on common equity of 15% with a 37% dividend payout ratio will mean a growth rate of common equity from plowback of retained earnings of 9.5%.

Exhibit 4–1

**Growth, in Keeping with Common Equity
Growth from Retained Earnings**
(In Millions)

Balance Sheet

Line	Assets	Year 1 Beginning	Year 1 Ending or Year 2 Beginning	
1	Current Assets	$100	$109.5	
2	Plant, Net	50	54.8	
3	Total Assets	$150	$164.3	

Line	Liabilities	Year 1 Beginning	Year 1 Ending or Year 2 Beginning	
4	Current Liabilities	$ 50	$ 54.8	
	Long-Term Capital			
5	Debt	27	29.6	27%
6	Common	73 + $6.9 + 9.5% ------>	79.9	73
7	Total Capital	$100	$109.5	100%
8	Total Liabilities	$150	$164.3	

Income Statement

Line		Year 1	
9	Sales	$200.0	
10	Operating Expenses		
11	Income Before Interest and Taxes		
12	Interest		9.5% Increase
13	Income After Interest Before Taxes		Produced by
14	Income Taxes		15% Earnings on
15	Net Income ($73 Common x 15% Earnings on common)	$ 11.0	Common x63% Retention
16	Dividends (37% payout)	4.1	
17	Earnings Retained (63% Retention)	$ 6.9	

With this increase in common equity, long-term debt can be increased 9.5% and still keep a 27% debt ratio. This will increase total long-term capital by $9.5 million, of which $6.9 million will come from retained earnings and $2.6 million from additional debt capacity.

If current assets and current liabilities are kept in the same relative size to long-term capital, then total assets and liabilities will increase at 9.5%.

Other important ratios will also be in line if your company keeps these three ratios in line.

GROWTH IN SALES AND PROFIT MARGIN

Sales growth has to be related to capital. In our example, sales were $200,000,000 and common capital was $73,000,000. Thus, $1.00 of common capital was needed to generate $2.74 of sales. If this same relationship holds in the future, then sales can grow at 9.5% since capital will grow at 9.5%.

Net income of $11,000,000 in year 1 represents a profit margin of 5.5% on $200,000,000 of sales. Since net income and sales will each increase at 9.5%, the 5.5% profit margin will remain constant.

The so-called DuPont formula shows how the profit margin is tied to capital turnover and how, together, they produce return on capital. Competitive pressure on margins can be offset by better capital turnover. In applying the DuPont formula, various figures may be used for capital. In the example which follows, we have used common equity with corresponding income.

$$\frac{Sales}{Common\ Capital} \times \frac{Return}{Sales} = \frac{Return}{Common\ Capital}$$

$$\frac{\$200,000,000}{\$\ 73,000,000} \times \frac{\$\ 11,000,000}{\$200,000,000} = \frac{\$11,000,000}{\$73,000,000}$$

$$\$2.74 \qquad\qquad 5.5\% \qquad = \qquad 15\%$$

COVERAGE OF INTEREST CHARGES

As we have previously said, the quality of a bond and its rating depend on the earnings protection afforded by income as expressed by the number of times interest charges are covered by pre-tax income. If your company has the proper ratio of debt to total long-term capital and a good return on common equity, it has to follow that interest will be well protected by earnings.

We can show this by using the figures in Exhibit 4–1. If we leave off the millions, in year 1 your company had $100 in long-term capital of which $27 was in debt and $73 in common, and since it earned 15% on the common, the income available for the common would be $11.00 as in Exhibit 4–1.

We can then build up the pre-tax income and coverage as follows:

Income available for common ($73 x 15%)	$11.0
Income taxes at 40% effective rate	7.3
Income before income taxes after interest	$18.3
Interest on bonds ($27 x 8%) plus $0.4 for an assumed amount of interest on bank loans	$ 2.6
Income before interest and income taxes	$20.9
Pre-tax coverage of interest charges	$\dfrac{\$20.9}{\$\ 2.6} = 8x$

This is a strong coverage, and would permit a small industrial company to have fine credit, a moderate sized company to be a strong A, and a large well situated industrial company to be a strong AA rating.

CASH FLOW FOR LONG-TERM DEBT

Another important ratio which the rating agencies consider in determining a bond rating for most types of companies is cash flow as a percent of long-term debt.

One of the principal items in cash flow is the non-cash expense of depreciation. Net income available for common is also considered part of cash flow in this financial ratio even though cash may be used for dividends. In our example in Exhibit 4–1, we had $27 of long-term debt and net income of $11.0. Depreciation of an industrial company might represent 3% of sales which would mean $6.0 in our example.

Thus total cash flow would be as follows:

Depreciation	$6.00
Net Income for common	11.0
Total cash flow	$17.0

$$\frac{\text{Cash flow}}{\text{Long term debt}} = \frac{\$17.0}{\$27.0} = 63\%$$

This is an excellent figure for an industrial company.

APPLICATION TO VARIOUS TYPES OF COMPANIES

In our discussion regarding the three key ratios, we used for illustrative purposes an industrial company which would be small for bond rating purposes. However, the same ideas apply to all sizes and types of companies. For example, a large independent finance company, depending on the nature of business, might be able to have debt equal to 80% or 85% of total long-term capital because the risk is low compared to a typical industrial company. Interest charges would be large because of the large debt, and pre-tax coverage of interest charges consequently would be much lower than for an industrial company. However, if the company earned 15% on its common equity, the pre-tax coverage would be between 1½x and 2x which should be adequate to provide quality rating for its senior debt.

Commerical banking is quite different from most types of business, but properly established, the three ratios also apply to banking. The equity ratio to total capital should be established as a percent of all deposits, non-subordinated debt, subordinated debt and equity. The proper amount of equity depends on the nature of a bank's assets and its earning ability. One reason the banking industry failed so miserably to keep an adequate equity was because the equity ratio was measured as a percent of subordinated debt plus equity—a superficial approach. This was promoted by many investment bankers and sanctioned by some bank regulators.

The profitability of a bank can be measured in terms of return on earning assets, on total assets, as well as on common equity. In 1977, all insured commerical banks[1] had common equity equal to 7% of total liabilities. Net income was 0.8% on average total assets, and 11.7% on average equity. However, the point is that you have to work from return on common with a sound amount of common to establish the appropriate return on assets and earning assets. And furthermore, return on common with a sound amount of common is the best test of a bank's earning ability to protect its debt. Coverage of interest charges for subordinated debt is highly leveraged and coverage of total interest charges is so small that it is hard to distinguish between an adequate and inadequate figure.

CONCLUSION

Of course, income statements and balance sheets do not move as smoothly as our simple example. However, we hope you are convinced that the three ratios we covered in Chapters 1, 2, and 3 are the ones with which you should be most concerned and that they will determine the future of your company regardless of its type because everything else has to fall in line.

---

[1]Federal Deposit Insurance Corporation Annual Report 1977.

Chapter 5

IS INVESTOR RELATIONS WORTHWHILE?

Your attitude toward investor relations may be colored by your experience. Investors relations can be stimulating if your company is doing well, the market is bullish and analysts are eager to recommend your stock. You may feel that it is a drag if you have been doing it for a long time through favorable and unfavorable conditions. You may feel totally frustrated if your company is doing well, but the market is dull, investors have no interest in your stock and your stock is selling for a very low price-earnings ratio. You may feel like avoiding it if your company is doing poorly.

These are all natural reactions. For this reason, we will first answer the questions we raised about investor relations in the Introduction. Is it an obligation? Is it worthwhile?

IS IT AN OBLIGATION?

A common stockholder in a publicly owned company has to purchase his stock in the market and he has to sell it in the market to get his money back. He should have the opportunity to buy and sell it at a fair price. A fair price is dependent on the market place having complete, pertinent information. Therefore, investor relations is an obligation for a publicly owned company.

IS IT WORTHWHILE?

Investor relations should be worthwhile because the return an investor requires depends on his appraisal of risk. Lack of information and, even more important, misinformation, adds to an investor's appraisal of risk. Therefore, providing complete information should reduce the investor's appraisal of risk and produce a better price for your company's stock in the long run. There may be other advantages. It may make it easier to raise capital. It may make it easier to get investors to agree to changes in security terms and charter provisions. It may help if you are faced with a takeover by another company. Thus, it should be worthwhile if your company is going to be a viable entity in the market.

WHAT PART SHOULD YOU PLAY?

The job of developing and running your company's investor relations program, will, of course, be delegated to someone in your company. However, you will have an important part to play even though limited. Your part is in three areas:

1. Setting the tone your company takes in investor relations.
2. Appearing before investor groups.
3. Delegating the responsibility for investor relations to the right executive and monitoring it.

SETTING THE TONE

What is meant by setting the tone your company takes can best be explained by stating the purpose of investor relations:

THE PURPOSE OF INVESTOR RELATIONS SHOULD BE TO COMMUNICATE PROMPTLY TO ALL THOSE IN-TERESTED ALL INFORMATION HAVING AN EFFECT ON YOUR COMPANY'S SECURITIES, BOTH FAVORABLE AND UNFAVORABLE, SO THAT YOUR COMPANY'S SECURITIES CAN BE EVALUATED ON THE BASIS OF COMPLETE IN-FORMATION.

The importance of giving out both favorable and unfavorable information cannot be over emphasized. That is the way you build credibility, the key word; that is the tone you have to set. If you don't build credibility, investors will not believe in your favorable de-velopments and will fear the worst when things go wrong.

There are some chief executive officers who are so constituted that they cannot direct a satisfactory investor relations program. In this group are the promoter types, who own some of their company's stock and want to push up the price. There were a number of conglomerateers in this category in the 1960's. Unfortunately for our free enterprise system some of the worst ones are still around and new ones still rear their ugly heads. It is only a question of time before they lose credibility and ultimately their stocks will suffer.

Also in this group of chief executive officers who treat investor relations incorrectly are those who have come up through sales and can't take off their sales hat. They tend to relate investor relations to public relations; even if their ship is sinking, they still do their optimistic pitch. The fact is that investor relations and public rela-tions are far apart. Investor relations is not a promotion operation; it is an information function. In order for the sales type of person to participate effectively in meetings with investors, he should cover operating and management aspects and let the financial vice-president cover the financial story.

The following example indicates the wrong attitude of management. A company discovers that a previous acquisition is a turkey and should be sold. How can it be sold at a loss without showing the loss on its books? What clever accounting or financial scheme can be devised to handle the situation? If the company were privately owned, would the professional manager try to deceive its sole owner? Obviously not! Why should the professional manager do any differently for a large number of stockholders? The fact is that the company lost money on the acquisition and the stockholders should be told the truth. This is the kind of philosophy we need in order for free enterprise to have credibility. Graduate business schools need to ridicule such chicanery. Directors should object. And accounting firms should refuse to give an unqualified audit. But unfortunately we have a way to go as regards some managements, directors, graduate schools and accountants.

What you say during favorable conditions should be tested on the basis of whether you would emphasize the same points under unfavorable conditions. For example, last year—"Earnings were excellent with earnings per share up 10%." Would you be just as forthright when earnings decreased? "Earnings were poor with earnings per share off 10%." Here is an actual example of the first paragraph in an honest letter to stockholders in an annual report:

> The year was disappointing in many respects. The weather was moderate most of the year which adversely affected revenues. Much needed rate relief was too little and too late in the year to significantly alter utility earnings. Our cost of gas purchased for resale soared 75 percent over last year's cost and additional revenues did not adequately offset the expenses. As a result our utility income dropped 49 percent.

In discussing the public's poor image of corporations, Alexander S. Kroll, president of Young & Rubican USA[1] commented on self regulation as follows: "Self regulation is no mere side show on the

---

[1]"Feedback on Corporate Images," by Philip H. Dougherty. © 1977 by the New York Times Company. Reprinted by permission.

fringe of business. It's a necessary prerequisite for saving business. We must impose limits upon ourselves or limitations will be imposed on us."

This thought certainly applies to the tone you should set for your company on investor relations.

MAKING APPEARANCES

The second part you have to play is appearing before certain groups of investors such as security analysts. The number of appearances will depend upon the size of your company and the investor interest. Management is an important consideration in evaluating a security and your presentation will show the extent of your grasp of your company's operations and also your understanding of what investors want to know. You may prefer to play only a part in the presentations and have some of your other executives cover various subjects. However, the way it is orchestrated in terms of a balanced presentation will be looked upon as your responsibility. A rehearsal is worthwhile if you are new at the game and you might have someone critique it who is familiar with the operation.

If your company has stock held abroad it may be worthwhile to have meetings with foreign investors. It will generally be done with the aid of an investment banker and with you in attendance.

DELEGATING THE RESPONSIBILITY

Our third point about your part in investor relations has to do with the person to whom you delegate the job of running the program. We feel that it should be under the direction of your financial vice-president. He should be the best equipped to get across the financial story of your company on a creditible basis. If your company is large enough to have a specialist in investor relations, he should report to the financial vice-president. Some companies split up their investor relations work. For example, communication with analyst may be done by a company's financial officer and the annual report under public relations. Many annual reports have been spoiled by public relations people. This is an observation over a forty year period and there has been no indication that things have changed. Some public relations people seem to be obsessed with putting out a bullish document which emphasizes the favorable developments and glosses over the unpleasant facts—a glorification of management's achievements. *That is not investor relations!* Your public relations experts certainly should have a part to play, but they should be directed and not direct. Some laughable results have occurred in annual reports as a consequence of public relations people getting the upper hand. For example, one annual report had a small picture of the president in different poses at the beginning of each paragraph of the president's letter. It isn't hard to guess who the public relations people were trying to please—certainly not the stockholders.

In the rest of this chapter, we will comment briefly on:

A progam for your company.
Who should be cultivated.
When an analyst says sell your stock.
A few additional ideas on your annual report.
Whether you should forecast earnings.
Contacting the rating agencies.
Some rules for your directors.

A PROGRAM

As we have already suggested, the extent of your program will depend on the size of your company and the extent of investor interest and also on your interest in the subject. The important point is to have a program, whether large or small, and make it continuous and consistent. If you put on a large display when things are favorble and then withdraw when things are unfavorable, you will lose creditability.

WHO SHOULD BE CULTIVATED?

One consideration in developing a program depends on whom you decide to cultivate. There are two groups of investors, the so-called informed and the uninformed. We use the words "so-called" because so many of them are lacking in adequate skills necessary to advise the poor uninformed investors what to buy and sell, but you can't do much about that.

In order to make a considered judgment regarding whether to buy or sell a security, the following background is required as a start: courses in accounting, courses in corporate finance, and concentrated training in analyzing securities. The uninformed include the investors who have none of these skills. They don't know the difference between a balance sheet and an income statement. All you can hope to do directly for the uninformed is in a one or two page letter to your stockholders in your annual report say something about earnings per share, dividends per share and the health of your company.

It is ridiculous to believe that by having your public relations expert jazz up your annual report you are going to help the uninformed investor. The uninformed investor has to rely on the informed investor to decide whether to buy or sell. Thus, your primary audience has to be the informed group, the financial analysts and securities dealers.

WHEN AN ANALYST SAYS SELL YOUR STOCK

When you see a report by a financial analyst recommending sale of your company's stock, you may feel that he is totally wrong and is doing your company a disservice. You, of course, have a right to be annoyed if he makes mistakes about the facts. However, he must call the shots as he sees them. His obligation is to the investors and he cannot compromise this obligation for any reason. With a change in your company's financial results, or a change in the market price, this same analyst may be recommending purchase of your stock.

There continues to be some misunderstanding by management regarding the position of financial analysts in a firm which does both investment banking and brokerage business. Some chief executive officers doing investment banking business with a firm become offended when the analysts servicing the brokerage business write adverse reports or ignore them altogether. In order to avoid any conflict of interest, analysts servicing the brokerage business must be independent of the corporate finance department handling the investment banking business.

Some investment bankers try to get the new business by suggesting that their research department follows the company's stock. That is not ethical and you should not want them on your team.

The corporate finance department may write what is known as a progress report about your company. This is done independently of the research department as a service to your company. An experienced financial analyst should realize that this may be a biased report and should be used mainly for factual material.

YOUR ANNUAL REPORT

Your annual report is your most important means of communication with investors. It is the report of your financial stewardship of your company, and that is what it should be—a complete report of what happened financially and why—that is the theme, this year, next year and every year. Some annual reports have one theme one year and another theme another year. As a result they do not give a balanced financial story.

By looking at your annual report an investor should be able to get some idea of your company's attitude about investor relations. Characteristics which an annual report should have are:

Completeness

It should tell all the story each year. Some companies feel that if they have covered a subject in the previous year, they don't have to cover it this year. Wrong! the reader does not want to have to go back to a previous report to get a complete story.

Balance

The amount of space given to each subject should be related to its importance as regards the company's securities.

Analytical Quality

Figures and narrative should be able to be used for analyzing the company's securities. A statement that wages increased, without the percent increase and the date, is of no analytical value. As another example, a statement such as, "an important division had a favorable year" has no analytical value. Figures should show the importance of the division and the actual or percent improvement.

Readability

Most annual reports test hard to read. If you don't believe it, have yours tested by a standard readability test.[2] Because of the contents, you probably can't make your annual report very easy to read, but

---

[2]A readability test is included in *The Art of Readable Writing* by Rudolph Flesch. Revised 1974 by Harper and Row Publishers, Inc., New York.

you should give it a try. This is where your public relations people might be able to help.

So many people get their fingers in writing most annual reports it is a wonder that they are comprehensible. As we have said it should be under the direction of the financial vice-president with the assistance of the public relations officer and not vice versa.

If yours is a complicated company, your financial vice-president should weigh the advisability of also issuing a statistical book. You should expect that this will require considerable work to make it well done. It should represent a complete story with tables and written material.

GIVING OUT FORECAST EARNINGS PER SHARE

One of the most difficult decisions you will have to make in investor relations is what policy you will follow with regard to forecasting earnings per share. Many analysts will pressure you into doing so. However, you should weigh the dangers. If your earnings per share are $2.50 and you forecast $3.00 for next year, you will be a hero if they turn out to be $3.00. However, if your earnings turn out to be $2.50 instead of $3.00, the analysts will be looking for someone to blame for having recommended your stock. You will be the goat. This is the easiest way to lose that important ingredient of investor relations—credibility.

Be liberal with the information you give analysts, but don't take the final step and forecast earnings. You can explain errors in your forecast of sales, etc., but not that final figure of earnings per share.

Some companies give analysts an indication of earnings per share by saying what most analysts are forecasting. In our opinion, this is just about the same as giving a forecast figure because you wouldn't mention it if it didn't agree with your estimate. And if that is the situation, you may be giving out inside information which should be put on the ticker for all to see.

If you don't give out forecast earnings per share, you may wonder what to do with an analyst who shows you his forecast which is way off the mark. If you do nothing you may fear that some investors will be mislead. Many companies in such a situation will try to get the analyst pointed in the right direction by suggesting that he review the basis for his forecast. On the other hand, if you do too much you may in effect be giving him your forecast.

Some companies take a very strict approach in this situation and tell analysts that they will help them with any facts, but that they will not comment in any way on their earnings per share forecast. They make it clear that that is the analysts' responsibility and very rightly so. We feel that it is the soundest approach in the long run.

CONTACTING THE RATING AGENCIES

The rating you receive on your bonds by the rating agencies is the record of your financial standing for the world to see. It affects your ability to raise capital and the interest rate you pay. Keeping the rating agencies informed is a very important part of your investor relations program. Some companies do a mediocre or poor job in their relations with the rating agencies. Errors that are made include:

Fear of seeing the agencies because earnings are poor.
Not seeing them on a regular basis.
Playing games as to what to present.
Poorly prepared presentation.

There is only one way to handle the rating agencies to get the best results in the long run, and that is as follows:

See them on a regular basis
Be very well prepared when you see them.

Give them all the facts, both good and bad.

Keep them currently informed of important developments.

It is sad to watch some companies in meetings with the agencies trying to do a sales job rather than providing information. You can see the rating people getting uneasy because they feel that they are being given a snow job. After the meeting, the company people may be heard to remark that the meeting helped build their credibility—they know the buz word, but they don't know the difference between trying to sell credibility and being credible.

Your principal aim should be to build complete confidence and trust in your management so that when your company has a downturn and you believe things will pick up, the agencies will believe you.

Before you have a meeting with the rating agencies it is advisable to rehearse your presentation.

There are two schools of thought with regard to the written material you should prepare. One school suggests a limited amount so the agencies will not be snowed under. The other school suggests preparing a large notebook which covers every possible subject that might be of interest. We believe that the latter approach is to be preferred. If you have the notebook prepared with an index, the rating agency analysts can readily turn to what they want to cover. In making an appearance, you may only refer to some of the material, but if the agency representatives ask questions which you did not mention in your presentation, you are in an excellent position to answer them by referring to the explanation in the notebook. Without any written material on the subject, you may give the appearance that you tried to avoid the subject.

The first time your company prepares a notebook for the rating agencies, it is a sizable task. Your financial officer should give one of his bright young men ample time to prepare it. It can include confidential material because the agencies will use it for rating purposes only. Once the task has been completed it can easily be kept up-to-date.

The written material should be sent to the rating agencies sufficiently prior to your meeting so that they will have a chance to study it.

Some investment bankers may suggest that through their contacts with the rating agencies that they can help you get a better rating. Wrong! A good investment banker should be in close contact with the agencies and know their concerns and should be able to help you get well prepared to present a total story. However, to intimate that an inside track can help obtain a better rating is not true.

If you think your securities should have their rating increased, it is terribly frustrating if the rating agencies do not make the change. However, the rating agencies want their ratings to be reasonably permanent. Therefore, they want to see an improved record, not just a recent improvement and a good forecast. In spite of your frustration, don't let it get you down and become too pushy with the agencies. Their only interest is in giving you the right rating because their obligation is to the investors. There is no benefit to them from assigning too low a rating. Remember that if your results are poor for a moderate period of time, they likewise will not rate your securities down.

DIRECTORS

We said in our discussion of dividend policy that this is one of the best investor relations tools. The make-up of the Board of directors is another investors relations tool; they are supposed to represent the stockholders.

A board of directors performs many functions, but the most important one is to choose and remove the chief executive officer, particularly the latter function. There is no one else who can do that job except the board; that is the place where the buck stops. In order to be effective, there are certain rules that should be applied. The board must be made up of outsiders. With an eleven man board, there should be no more than two inside members since the inside members are going to vote for management. No board member should receive any business from the company in order to avoid any conflict of interest. The buddy system of you on my board and me on your board should not be tolerated. New board members should be chosen by a committee of outside members of the board. The audit committee should be made up of outside members. Once a year, the outside members should meet separately to discuss the management of the company and then should review their thoughts with the management.

A board of directors should not attempt to manage the company, but should study the management decisions sufficiently so that they are convinced there is good management.

If the company is well managed it doesn't make much difference how the board is made up. However, if the company becomes poorly managed, there is little likelihood that anything will be done about it unless a board functions with the rules suggested above.

You might only want to be on a board so constituted, otherwise you will not be able to carry out your obligation to the shareholders whom you represent. And top management should not want any other type of board because they should be sufficiently confident to withstand proper scrutiny.

We previously quoted a statement to the effect that if management doesn't regulate itself, regulation will be imposed on it. Improvement of boards of directors to truly represent the stockholders is so long overdue that no one should complain if the government steps in and sets the rules.

CONCLUSION

So much for an overview of your part in investor relations. The key words are "Let it all hang out" and "credibility." You shouldn't want the providers of capital to receive other than a fair return in keeping with the risk based on all the facts. And if you try to do otherwise you will be adding to investors evaluation of risk. If your company were privately owned by one person, you, as the professional manager, would be expected to keep him fully informed. Your responsibility is just as great to public stockholders.

Some of the first securities laws were passed by states to protect investors. They were known as "blue sky laws" because they were for the purpose of protecting investors from being sold the blue sky. Companies now feel that they are overburdened with laws designed to keep investors informed. In reality it is not that difficult if a company sincerely has in mind telling investors all the facts. Business has come a long way since the first blue sky laws were passed, but there is still a way to go.

Chapter 6

HOW YOUR COMPANY'S EARNINGS PER SHARE GROW AND A SATISFACTORY PRICE FOR YOUR STOCK

You cannot use the effect on current earnings per share for making financial and capital management decisions. Current earnings per share may be increased in various ways which would subsequently produce unsatisfactory results. For example, leverage increases current earnings per share, but carried too far it is unsound. As another example, under some circumstances capital may be put to work below the economic cost of capital and increase current earnings per share. This would be an unsound policy. Return on investment and not earnings per share should be used for such decisions.

Even though you can't use earnings per share for decision-making, you will want to weigh the effect of your decisions on earnings per share. Because investors follow earnings per share, changes in earnings per share may have an immediate effect on the market price of your stock. Under certain circumstances, you may decide against a project which would be satisfactory except for the effect on current earnings per share. Your decision will have to be a trade-off of the long range benefit of the project on your company's stock vs the adverse short range effect.

For these reasons you will want to know how earnings per share change. In the first part of the chapter, we will cover this subject; in the second part, we will explain what is meant by a satisfactory price for your stock.

GROWTH IN EARNINGS PER SHARE

The five ways earnings per share grow are:

1. PLOWBACK OF EARNINGS.
2. INCREASE IN RETURN ON COMMON EQUITY.
3. SALE OF COMMON STOCK ABOVE BOOK VALUE.
4. HIGH PRICE-EARNINGS RATIO COMPANY AC-QUIRES LOWER PRICE-EARNINGS RATIO COM-PANY.
5. REPURCHASE OF COMMON STOCK.

1. Plowback of Earnings

We have already explained in Chapter 3 on dividend policy how plowback of earnings increases earnings per share. So that you won't have to turn back to that chapter, we will review it briefly.

The rate of increase depends on the amount of earnings retained, which is the balance left after dividend payments, and on the rate earned on the additional capital. The formula is:

$$\left\{\begin{array}{l}\text{\% Earned on}\\\text{Beginning}\\\text{Common}\\\text{Book Value}\end{array}\right\} \times \left\{\begin{array}{l}\text{\% of Earnings}\\\text{Retained (100\% minus}\\\text{percent of Earnings paid}\\\text{out in dividends)}\end{array}\right\} = \left\{\begin{array}{l}\text{Growth Rate}\\\text{in Earnings}\end{array}\right\}$$

The simplest example we used was a company earning 10% on its beginning common book value and expecting to continue to earn the same rate. It paid out 50% of its earnings in dividends and retained the other 50%. Therefore, the growth rate in earnings per share would be 10% × 50% = 5%. And the book value per share and dividends per share will also increase at the same rate.

In Chapter 3, we showed growth rates with various returns and payouts, with dividends at 5% and 6% on beginning book value. In this chapter, we will use dividends at half way between these two figures, that is, at 5.5%.

Exhibit 6–1 shows growth rates with this dividend policy. These growth rates are meaningful, because they are sustainable as long as the returns are maintained. Remember that in order to maintain the growth rates, the return on both the old and new capital must be maintained.

If the price-earnings ratio of a stock remains constant then the market price of the stock would increase at the same rate as the earnings increase. In the exhibit, this would mean market appreciation of 7.5%, 9.5% and 11.5%.

Exhibit 6–1

Increase in Earnings Per Share From Plowback, with Constant Dividend as a Percent of Book Value and Constant Return On Common Book Value

Line				
1	Return on beginning book value	13%	15%	17%
2	Dividends as percent of beginning book value	5.5%	5.5%	5.5%
3	Dividend payout ratio	42%	37%	32%
4	*Increase in earnings per share*	7.5%	9.5%	11.5%
5	Market appreciation with a constant price-earnings ratio	7.5%	9.5%	11.5%

2. Increase in Return

If a company paid out all of its earnings in dividends, or in other words, had a 100% dividend payout policy, there would be no growth in earnings per share from plowback. However, earnings of such a company would grow if the return on the common book value increases.

For example, if a company has a book value of $100 per share and earns 13% on the book value, it will earn $13 per share. With a 100% payout policy, the dividend would be $13. There would be no growth from plowback. If next year it earned 14% on book value, the earnings per share would be $14 which would be a 7.7% increase in earnings per share. These figures are shown in Exhibit 6-2. If the price-earnings ratio remains constant, the market price will increase 7.7%.

Exhibit 6-2

**Increase in Earnings Per Share
From Increase in Return on Common Book Value**

Return on Beginning Common Book Value 13% in Year 1, Increasing to 14% in year 2. All Earnings Paid out in Dividends

Line		Year 1	Year 2
1	Beginning common book value per share	$100	$100
2	Return on beginning book value	13%	14%
3	Earnings per share	$13	$14
4	Less: dividend—100% paid out	13	14
5	Retained earnings	0	0
6	*Increase in earnings per share*	—	7.7%
7	Market price (price-earnings ratio = 7.7x)	$100.10	$107.78

As a result of an increase in the return on common book value, a company may be able to show a substantial increase in earnings per share for a few years, particularly if it starts with a low rate of return. This may be the principal way in which earnings per share of a new company grows for a fairly sustained period. For example, a new company may show returns of 3%, 4%, 5%, 6%, etc. in successive years, which would provide a high growth rate.

The stock market may misinterpret such growth and regard the company as a true growth company. However, there is some point at which the return on common book value must level off, depending on the nature of the company's business, competition, etc. Accordingly, we do not regard growth in earnings per share resulting from an increase in return as indicative of the sustainable growth of a company. The true long-range growth rate depends on the typical rate of return that the company can maintain over the long run and the dividend payout policy.

3. Sale of Common Stock Above Book Value

We will assume that a company offers 1/10 of a new share for each one share outstanding, or a 10% increase in shares. We will also assume that the stock is sold at 131% of book value, and at 7.7 times earnings. Since the stock is sold above book value, the book value per share increases and, if the same return is earned, earnings per share increase. These figures are shown in Exhibit 6–3. Earnings per share increased 2.8%.

This, of course, does assume that the same return is earned on the new investment as on the old investment.

If stock is sold below book value and the return is the same, earnings per share would decrease. Continuous sale of stock below book value will erode earnings per share.

Exhibit 6–3

**Increase in Earnings per Share From
Sale of Stock Above Book Value**

1-for-10 Offering

Sell 1/10 of a new share for each share outstanding at a market price 131% of beginning common book value. Return on new capital same as on existing capital.

Line		Before Sale of Common	After Sale of Common
1	Beginning common book value	$100.00	$100.00
2	1/10 of a new share sold at market price of $131.	—	13.10
3	Total book value	$100.00	$113.10
4	Shares outstanding	1	1.1
5	Book value per share	$100.00	$102.82
6	Return on common book value	17%	17%
7	Earnings per share	17.00	17.48
8	Less: dividends—100% paid out	17.00	17.48
9	Retained earnings	0.00	0.00
10	*Increase in earnings per share*	—	2.8%
11	Market price (price-earnings ratio = 7.7x)	$130.90	$134.60

4. High P/E Ratio Company Acquires Lower P/E Ratio Company

If an acquiring company's price-earnings ratio is higher than the price-earnings ratio of a company acquired, then current earnings per share will increase. This is illustrated by the simple figures in Exhibit 6–4, with both companies the same size. The acquired company is selling for 7.7 times earnings. The acquiring company

Exhibit 6–4

**Increase in Earnings Per Share From
High Price-Earnings Ratio Company
Acquiring Lower Price-Earnings Company**

Line		Company A The Acquiring Company	Company B
1.	Income for Common	$100	$100
2.	Shares outstanding	10	10
3.	Earnings per share	$ 10	$ 10
4.	Loss: dividends—100% paid out	$ 10	$ 10
5.	Retained earnings	0	0
6.	Price-earnings ratio	10x	7.7x
7.	Market price	$100	$ 77
8.	Shares issued by Company A to acquire Company B on the basis of market prices[1]	7.7	

		Company A after Acquiring Company B
9.	Income for Common	$200.00
10.	Shares outstanding	17.7
11.	Earnings per share	$ 11.30
12.	*Increase in earnings per share*	13%
13.	Price-earnings ratio[2]	10x
14.	Market price	$113

[1]No allowance is made for a premium for the exchange in order to keep the exhibit simple.
[2]This assumes that investors evaluate the combined earnings at the same price-earnings ratio as the acquiring company.

happens to sell at a higher price-earnings ratio because investors consider the outlook more favorable. As a result of the transaction, current earnings per share increase 13%.

This is a one shot type of earnings per share increase. In order to keep it going, there has to be a continuous stream of acquisitions.

This is the reason the market price of many conglomerates collapsed after the merger boom of the 1960's came to a halt.

5. Repurchase of Common Stock

If the after-tax return on the funds used to repurchase common stock is less than the earnings-price ratio, current earnings per share will increase.

Exhibit 6–5 shows a simple example of a company which repurchased 10% of its stock. It used idle cash which was not earning anything. In such a situation, as long as the company earns something on its common stock, current earnings per share will increase as a result of the repurchase.

Exhibit 6–5

Increase in Earnings per Share from Repurchase of Common Stock

The total common book value before purchase is represented by assets consisting of $10 cash and $90 of earning assets, with 10 shares of stock outstanding. The $10 of cash is used to purchase 1 share of common stock at book value.

Line		Before Purchase	After Purchase
1	Total common book value represented by:		
	Cash	$ 10	
	Earning assets	90	$90
	Total	$100	$90
2	Total earnings	$ 13	$13
3	Number of shares	10	9
4	Earnings per share	$1.30	$1.44
5	Less: dividends—100% paid out	1.30	1.44
6	Retained earnings	0.00	0.00
7	*Increase in earnings per share*	0	10.8%
8	Market price (price-earnings ratio=7.7x)	$100.10	$110.88

Simply because current earnings per share can be increased by repurchase of stock does not necessarily justify the repurchase of common stock. The pros and cons of such transactions were commented on in Chapter 3.

SUMMARY OF GROWTH IN EARNINGS PER SHARE

As we have emphasized, there is only one way in which earnings per share increase so as to provide a sustainable rate of increase. That is through plowback. All the others are transitory. This is not to say that such increases are necessarily the result of unsound policies. They may or they may not be.

Actual growth in earnings per share in any one year depends on how quickly new capital is put to work. Also, it may be the result of one or more of the ways earnings per share grow which take place in varying degree during the year, rather than at the beginning of the year as we have applied the figures. Therefore it may be difficult to separate them. But in the long run, the reason for the growth rate should be discernible.

The above five reasons for increasing earnings per share can also be used to describe how current earnings per share decrease when the reverse of these actions occur.

IS YOURS A GROWTH COMPANY?

From the point of view of investors, a growth company has to be measured in terms of the percent increase in earnings per share, not in increase in sales, assets or any other measure. There has never been a formal definition of what constitutes a growth company.

If a company earns a return of 13% on its common book equity, and the dividend payout ratio is 42% with dividends 5.5% on book value, the growth rate in earnings per share would be 7.5% from plowback. If the stock sold at book value, investors would get 5.5% from yield and 7.5% from market appreciation with a constant price-earnings ratio, or a total return 13%. If 13% is considered to be the common cost rate, then the company would be earning just the return investors required.

Thus we might suggest that the starting point for a growth company would be a growth rate in earnings per share of more than 7.5%.

However, without any qualifications, a definition of a growth company on the basis of growth in earnings per share may be meaningless. For example, earnings per share would grow at 7.5% if a company earned 10.00% on its book investment, paid out all of its earnings in dividends and increased the return by 7.5% to 10.75%. Or as another example, earnings per share would increase 7.5% if a company earned 7.5% on book equity and paid no dividends.

Therefore, in order to decide whether a company is truly a growth company in terms of earnings per share, you have to look at the reasons for the growth.

A far better test of a company's performance is the return on common equity with a sound capital structure. For a large company, we have suggested that around 13% might be breakeven, 15% good, and 17% excellent. These rates can then be translated into growth rates in earnings per share with a sound dividend policy. In this chapter, we showed in Exhibit 6–1 that for these returns with a dividend of 5.5% on beginning book, which might be within a range of being appropriate for certain types of industrial companies, the payout ratio and growth rates in earnings per share from plowback would be as follows:

Return on Beginning Common Book Value	Payout Ratio	Growth Rate in Earnings per Share
13%	42%	7.5%
15	37	9.5
17	32	11.5

A SATISFACTORY PRICE FOR YOUR STOCK

We have observed over many years that most chief executive officers feel that their company's stock is always underpriced no matter how high. The reason for such thinking may be that a competitor's stock is selling on a better basis and the competitor is inferior, particularly as regards management.

In spite of this normal reaction, you should be interested in what may be a reasonable price for your stock for three reasons:

1. Your company might be contemplating the sale of new stock, the use of stock for acquisitions or the repurchase of outstanding stock.
2. So that your stockholders will receive a fair return in keeping with your company's earning power.

   Too high a price may be as bad as too low, because if the price gets too high in relation to earning power, investors will receive less than a fair return and the price will have to fall. The ideal situation would be for the price-earnings ratio to remain constant relative to normalized earnings at a figure which will provide a fair return to stockholders in keeping with the return the company earns. As earnings per share grow from the plowback of earnings, the market price of the stock will appreciate.
3. To tell whether your investor relations program is effective.

In the 1960's with the crazy stock market many chief executive officers completely lost sight of the idea that there was such a thing as a reasonable price for their company's stock, and companies which were mismanaged and poor earners sold for ridiculous prices.

WHY MAY YOUR STOCK'S PRICE GET FAR OUT OF LINE?

Part of the reason your stock may get out of line is because rewards to stockholders come from future earnings, and stocks sell on the basis of what investors expect a company will earn. Past or current earnings are a clue as to future earnings, but not what make stock prices. In the 1960's investors were fantasizing.

If investors estimated future earnings per share on a long range basis from growth due to a company's basic earning power and the earnings retention rate, stock prices would tend to make more sense. Because investors are not frozen in when they buy a stock and think they can get out by selling if adversity appears, they may take a relatively short range view of a company's future earnings. And as we have explained, earnings per share may increase in the short run from various factors. This is really the greater fool theory of investing. An investor buys because he thinks a stock is going up. When he thinks it has reached its peak, he has to find someone to buy it who thinks it is going up further. If that fool doesn't turn up, he himself becomes the greater fool.

Many analysts act like lemmings. They look for hot stocks which will show an increase in near-term earnings per share. Each period has its glamor stocks which are in vogue while stocks of other companies with good basic performance may be ignored. The hotter a stock gets, the more analysts and brokers rush in and push it up. During a boom this action is particularly evident in the emphasis put on market appreciation rather than dividend yield. As the boom grows hotter, interest in dividend yield fades away. When the boom busts, the analysts all run for shelter. Thus, we have the irrational over-optimism and over-pessimism and the resulting extreme bull and bear markets.

There are a few fundamental analysts who look for value in terms of long-range earning power of a company. And there seem to be more thoughtful institutional investors taking this approach. However, these poor fellows may suffer badly in the short run because the market may ignore such values. They should come out ahead in the long run, but their praises may never be sung.

Some professors contend that the stock market is rational. Not so! Rational should mean that stock prices will provide investors a fair return in keeping with a company's ability to earn. The fact is that the market is only rational at times as it passes up or down.

As management, you can't do anything about this unfortunate situation, but it is important that you appreciate how irrational, at times, the market price of your stock may be. All you can do is console yourself with an understanding that these are the facts of life.

There are simple formulas which may help you decide what may be a reasonable price for your company's stock in the long run. They are based on the relationship of the return your company earns on the common stock book value and what investors want as a return on the market price and the relationship that should result between the market price of the stock and the common book value.

When we discuss growth in earnings per share in the following explanation, we will assume that it is due to plowback of earnings since this is the only way that earnings per share can grow continuously.

WHAT PRICE FOR YOUR STOCK IF ALL EARNINGS WERE PAID OUT IN DIVIDENDS?

In Chapter 2 we discussed the relationship of the return investors get on the market price and the return the company makes on the stockholders' investment. We will review this idea.

Remember we started with a company with a book value per share of $100 and earning $13 per share or 13% on book value. It is expected to earn this rate in the future. It pays out 100% of its earnings in dividends so that its dividend per share is $13. Since the company retains no earnings it will have no growth in earnings per share from plowback. We will call this Company A.

What should be the market price of Company A's stock? That depends on the yield that would satisfy investors. If investors wanted a 13% return on their money to induce them to buy the stock, then the market price should be $100 and the market price would be 100% of book value.

Suppose another company, B, had a book value per share of $100 and earned $26 per share or 26% on book value and paid a dividend of $26. If investors wanted a 13% return, the market price of the stock would be $200, so the stock would sell at 200% of book value.

These figures for Company A and B are summarized in Exhibit 6–6.

Exhibit 6–6

**Price of Stock for Companies Which Pay
Out All Their Earnings in Dividends**

Line		Company A	Company B
1	Book value per share	$100	$100
2	Return on book value	13%	26%
3	Earnings per share	$ 13	$ 26
4	Dividend Payout Ratio	100%	100%
5	Dividends per share	$ 13	$ 26
6	Return wanted by investors	13%	13%
7	Market price of stock	$100	$200

If all companies paid out all their earnings in dividends, determining the market price of a stock would be relatively easy. Investors would only have to figure out what the dividends were expected to be and what return they wanted. It isn't that easy, because most companies don't pay out all their earnings in dividends. Investors get their total return from dividends and market appreciation. How then might you evaluate the two parts in order to determine a market price for your company's stock?

Again, you would first have to decide how much total return investors might want from both the parts. So far in our examples above we have assumed that investors wanted a total return of 13%.

Before we go any further, we should repeat that investors might take a different attitude towards the two parts. Cash dividends are a bird in the hand and have no risk once they are received. In contrast, the value of the retained earnings depends on what the company does with them and how they are translated into market appreciation. We will ignore the distinction in the discussion which follows only to make it easier to understand.

Going back to Company A and B, suppose each paid out 50% of

their earnings in dividends. Company A, which earned 13% on its book value, would have an earnings per share growth of 6.5% because it would earn 13% on the 50% of retained earnings.

Company B, which earned 26% on its book value would have an earnings per share growth of 13% because it would earn 26% on the 50% of retained earnings. Investors would pay more for Company B's stock because the dividend was greater and also substantially more because it would earn more on the retained earnings.

So now we have to explain how to evaluate the price of a stock which does not pay out all of its earnings in dividends.

RETURN FROM MARKET APPRECIATION AND DIVIDEND YIELD

Market price appreciation can occur because of a change in earnings per share and also a change in the price-earnings ratio. The price-earnings ratio can go up and down, but it can't go in either direction indefinitely. Over the long run the price-earnings ratio should settle down at an average figure so that investors get a fair return in relation to the company's earnings. For our explanation, we will assume that the price-earnings ratio remains constant. If it does remain constant, then the percent return the investors get from market price appreciation will be the same as the percent increase in earnings per share. For example, if the earnings per share increased 10% from $10 to $11 and the price-earnings ratio remained constant at ten times, the market price would appreciate 10% from $100 to $110.

Let's assume that your company has a book value of $100 per share, earns 13% on beginning book value, and pays out 42% of earnings in dividends, what then should the stock sell for?

The growth rate in earnings per share would be 7.5% and the stockholders would get 7.5% from market appreciation with a constant price-earnings ratio.

We have assumed that common stockholders expected to get a return of 13%. If they get 7.5% from market appreciation, the balance of the return must come from dividend yield. By subtraction, the dividend yield would have to be 5.5%, that is, the 13% total return less the 7.5% market appreciation requires a dividend yield of 5.5%.

The dividend would grow at the same rate as the earnings and the market price of the stock; consequently the yield would remain constant.

Thus, for a company which has constant figures for rate of return, dividend payout ratio and price-earnings ratio, the total return to investors is equal to the growth rate in earnings per share plus the dividend yield.

These figures may be summarized as follows:

Total return expected by common stockholders	13.0%
Market appreciation. With a constant price-earnings ratio, it is the same as the growth rate in earnings per share.	7.5%
Dividend yield by subtraction. It remains constant if the payout is constant and the market price appreciates at the same rate as the earnings.	5.5%

PRICE-EARNINGS RATIO AND THE PRICE OF YOUR STOCK

In order to obtain the price-earnings ratio, we use the formula given below, the derivation of which is explained in Appendix IV, Part I

$$\text{Price-Earnings Ratio} = \frac{\text{Dividend Payout}}{\text{Dividend Yield}}$$

$$= \frac{42\%}{5.5\%}$$

$$= 7.7x$$

Before we come to a conclusion regarding the price of your stock we need to develop another ratio.

The relationship between market price and common book value is determined by the following formula, the derivation of which is also shown in Appendix IV, Part I.

Market Price Divided by Common Book Value	=	Return on Common Book Value x Price- Earnings Ratio
	=	13% x 7.7x
	=	100%

Thus, since the company's book value is $100, the stock should sell at 100% of book value or $100 per share to produce a 13% return for investors on the market price.

To summarize, a company should have a good idea of the long range growth rate in earnings per share from plowback which would provide a similar market appreciation for the stock with a constant price-earnings ratio. It should know what return investors require to induce them to put up common equity capital—this is the common cost rate. Subtracting the rate of market appreciation from the total return common stockholders want gives the dividend yield. Division of the yield into the payout gives the price-earnings ratio. Then, multiplying the price-earnings ratio by the long range return on book value gives the market price in the relationship to book value. The figures we have discussed are summarized in Exhibit 6–7.

LIMITATIONS OF FORMULAS

Unfortunately, we now have to tell you that the formulas do have definite limitations. They cannot be used if there is no yield, and they are sensitive to a low dividend. They are also sensitive to a change in the return required by investors. These limitations are explained in Appendix IV, Part II.

Exhibit 6–7

Return to Common Stockholders from Market Appreciation and Dividend Yield

Company earns 13% on Common Book Value of $100 per share, Pays Out 42% of Earnings in Dividends and Produces a 7.5% Growth Rate in Earnings and Dividends per Share from Plowback. No Other Factors Affect Growth in Earnings per Share.

Part I

Market Appreciation with Constant Price-Earnings Ratio

Line	Column	I	II	III	IV	V
		Earnings per Share	Growth Rate in Earnings per Share	Price-Earnings Ratio	Market Price Common	Appreciation in Market Price
	Year					
1	0	$13.00		7.7x	$100.00	
2	1	13.98	7.5%	"	107.50	7.5%

150

Part II
Dividend Yield with Constant Dividend Payout and Price-Earnings Ratio

Year	Earnings per Share	Dividend Payout Ratio	Dividends per Share	Price-Earnings Ratio	Market Price Common	Dividend Yield
0	$13.00	42%	$5.46	7.7x	$100.00	5.5%
1	13.98	"	5.87	"	107.50	"

Part III
Total Return to Common Stockholders

Market appreciation	7.5%
Dividend yield	5.5
Total return	13.00%

Part IV
Price-Earnings Ratio

$$\text{Price-earnings ratio} = \frac{\text{Payout}}{\text{Yield}}$$

$$= \frac{42\%}{5.5\%} = 7.7\text{x}$$

Part V
Market Price Divided by Book Value

Percent Return on Common Book Value × Price-Earnings Ratio = 13%x 7.7x = 100%

151

In spite of these limitations, the formulas may help you tie the whole picture together from what your company earns to what the investors get.

In considering what investors should pay for your stock ask yourself what picture you present to them.

1. What is the nature of your company's business? Is it a business in which investors should currently be interested? Is it clearly defined in related managable lines, or is it a conglomeration.

2. How risky is your business? Does its small size add to the risk? Is it over leveraged? Does it have a large foreign operation?

3. What has been your earnings record? Has it been variable? Have earnings been satisfactory in the last year or two? Is your return on capital high and vulnerable to being decreased by competition?

4. What have you shown investors about your faith in the company with your dividend record?

5. What has been your long range investor relations program? Do you project credibility or are you promoting your stock.

6. What managment picture do you present? Is your company well managed with depth of management and delegation of authority? Do you have proper goals for return on capital investment? Do you have a strong outside board?

Thus, with these factors in mind stand back and view your company as investors would view it. If you could get an 8% return on a good grade bond and should get a total return of around 13% to break even in a top quality stock of a very large company, how much total return should investors reasonably expect to get from your stock? Should it be 13%, 14%, 15% or more? Having come to an unbiased conclusion on this point, consider what investors might arrive at as a realistic return that your company might earn on an average over the long run based on the picture you present. This should help you arrive at a reasonable price for your stock which would be fair to your stockholders.

Chapter 7

WHAT YOU MIGHT EXPECT FROM YOUR FINANCIAL VICE-PRESIDENT

In this chapter, we will comment briefly on numerous additional financial subjects which will be handled by your financial vice-president. In Chapter 1, we suggested that you might wish to have a nodding acquaintance with them.

CORPORATE SET-UP

If yours is a company with a number of subsidiaries, the first decision that has to be made in financial planning is where financing should be done—in the subsidiaries, in the holding company, in both or in some subsidiaries and not in others. Should subsidiaries be set up for financing receivables or for real estate? Temporary expediency should not weigh heavily in this decision because it may be hard to reverse and could prove to be irreversible.

Some of the things companies do because of the apparent short range benefit was illustrated by the sale of minority interest in subsidiaries by a few companies in the 1960's. One of the purposes was supposedly to promote the price of the stock of the holding company. It was interesting to have watched the number of soberly run companies that wondered whether they should copy this idea. There may be a reason under special circumstances for the sale of a minority interest, but not to promote the price of the stock of the holding company.

FINANCIAL PLANNING AND TYPES OF SECURITIES

After the best corporate set-up has been established, the next step in financial planning is to lay out a five year financing program to raise the outside capital required in keeping with your company's goal for average and maximum debt to long-term capital.

Then you will have to select specific types of securities in these two broad categories. There are a great variety of debt securities with different security positions, terms and maturities. And there are different types of equity—preferred and common.

Your financial vice-president should have alternative plans to use if expected financing cannot be accomplished due to adverse markets or bad earnings.

Some types of securities have been badly misused. One of the worst examples was the use of convertible debentures to raise new money in the 1960's when common stock should have been sold. Convertibles are often touted on the superficial basis that they produce a low interest rate and a high price for your company's stock—totally false. Debentures with warrants attached have been misused in a similar fashion. However, used for the right purpose and at the right time, these securities may fill a need.

Some companies were convinced by leasing companies to lease instead of own, when the reverse would have been advisable. The result usually is a more costly form of debt financing. The changes in accounting for leases may help to reduce the misuse of leases. However, mistakes will continue to be made because there are some executives who don't understand what is meant by the debt equivalent cost of a lease.

Project financing is the indirect use of your company's credit, or the credit of a third party, or a combination of both. Payments to support the ultimate debt instrument may be based on contracts such as a take-or-pay agreement, an agreement to make whole, etc. The form of security which the institutional investors purchase is a debt instrument. Therefore, whoever's back the monkey is on to make the payments should consider the obligation a form of debt.

Your financial vice-president should know the terms for the various types of senior securities and how the terms may vary with different credit quality, with different market conditions, and with different ways securities are offered.

SELLING SECURITIES

In selling new senior securities, a decision may have to be made as to whether they should be sold privately or publicly. Regulated companies, such as utilities, will also have a choice as to whether to use competitive bidding.

Your financial vice-president should realize that investment bankers may prefer a private sale rather than a public offering. The compensation is less in a private sale, but the net profit may be greater because there is no underwriting risk, less time is required, and there is generally no sharing of income. He should choose an investment banking firm which has strong capability in either public offerings or private sales so that the firm's recommendation will not be prejudiced by its lack of ability to handle all methods of sale.

Some commerical banks act as agents in a private sale. However, your financial vice-president should consider the possible conflict of interest if the institution to which the placement is offered has a deposit in the bank. Deposits may be worth more to a bank than the commission in a private sale. Most commerical bankers do not do enough private sales to be highly skilled in terms. They may not have enough coverage to reach all buyers in the market to get the best rate. And they can only do private placements rather than

underwritten offerings so they may tend to push for private placements.

In selling common stock, your financial vice-president should
understand the relative merits of selling a stock directly or through
rights to existing stockholders. In the past many companies were
required to sell new stock through rights because of their charters.
Most companies have correctly eliminated this provision by amend-
ing their charters so that they can offer stock either directly or
through rights as best fits the circumstances. Because many companies used rights in the past, there were financial officers who knew
how to handle them. However, today it is somewhat of a lost art.
Your financial vice-president should realize that investment bankers
make less on rights offerings and are prejudiced against rights. They
may make the glib statement: "Don't use rights, the company gets
less net proceeds and the small stockholders take a licking." Not
necessarily so—it depends on many factors, perhaps the most important of which is the condition of the securities market.

If you should choose a rights offering, your financial vice-
president will need to answer many complicated questions such as:
where to set the subscription price, whether to have the issue
underwritten, whether to use a two fee or single fee method of
repaying underwriters, how to handle the tag end split, that is, the
profit on unsubscribed shares, and many other subtleties such as
oversubscription and dealer compensation.

In a direct offering of common stock, your financial vice-president
will have to decide such questions as whether to use a formula
method of pricing, which involves the method of establishing the
issue price; and whether to provide stock to the investment bankers
to take care of stock which they over-sell, the so-called Green Shoe
option.

With regard to selling securities in general, your financial vice-
president will have to negotiate with underwriters. He should be
knowledgeable in this area and well prepared so that he will not be
led around by the nose.

Be wary of an investment banker who pushes your company into the market because he expects the market will deteriorate. Generally, raise capital when you need it and don't try to outguess the market—do you know anyone who has been able to do so with any degree of consistency?

SHORT-TERM LOANS

Your financial vice-president should know how many banks to have and how to strike a proper balance in the use of short term funds between commercial banks and commerical paper. He should appreciate that the overuse of short term loans can place a company in a financial bind if markets become tight.

SPECIAL OPERATIONS

There are a number of special operations with which your financial vice-president may have to deal, such as: refunding senior securities, exchange offers for senior securities, calling convertibles, repurchase of common stock, purchase of bonds for sinking fund requirements, change in bond indenture provisions, stock splits, etc. All of these operations should be done with all pros and cons carefully considered.

Various parts of the financial community may touch on your company. For example, there is trading in options. Your financial vice-president may have to consider how it will affect the market price of your stock and how it might affect a new offering.

Arbitrage may occur in a convertible, an exchange offer, a rights offering, a tender offer, etc. Your financial vice-president may need to know its significance in these areas.

If your company is tendered for, your financial vice-president should know the three specialists to have immediately on tap—the underwriter, the legal specialist and the proxy soliciting firm. If he fails to have you and your directors prepared, you may not take appropriate actions which will be best for your stockholders.

If your company operates abroad, your financial officer will have to help keep exposure of capital investment to a minimum, reduce the adverse effect of currency fluctuations, handle tax aspects, and transfer funds to the U.S. And if you can raise capital abroad, your financial vice-president will have to know how to go about it.

If your company's stock is traded over-the-counter your financial vice-president will have to decide whether to list. And if your stock is listed, the exchange specialist should be regularly monitored by your financial vice-president. If your company has stock held abroad, the question of listing abroad may have to be determined.

RETURN ON INVESTMENT

We have indicated in our explanation of return on investment that its application to project analysis and division performance standards is one of the most difficult areas in finance. There are many on your team who should have an understanding of these subjects. Your financial vice-president should be able to play an important role in educating your team.

MANAGING SHORT-TERM INVESTMENTS

Your financial vice-president should supervise the investment of your excess cash. There are very few exceptions where he should try to increase the yield by investing in other than the highest grade investments with the shortest maturities. This is not an area for gamesmanship. For example, New York City bonds offered an enticing yield just before the City's credit collapsed.

FINANCIAL ADVISERS AND CHOICE OF AN
INVESTMENT BANKER

Your financial officer can't be expected to know all the subjects we have discussed, but he should know where to seek advice. He may find that management consultants are generally not skilled financial advisers.

Individual financial advisors may or may not be skilled, but they should be in the swim of things to keep sharp. Many professors are so wound up in their highly mathematical approaches to finance that they may have lost touch with the real world.

Some investment bankers are highly superficial and motivated by their desire to get a commission from the sale of a security. The right investment banker can be very helpful.

Picking an investment banker is an important decision so you will want to be involved. In the process, you may conduct what is called a "beauty contest." By a "beauty contest" is meant having a number of investment banking firms visit your company so they can tell you what they have to offer, or preferably you should visit them because then you may be able to see more people. After such a meeting you may make the wrong choice unless you are familiar with the investment banking business and question each investment banker carefully. The difficulty of making a choice arises because each investment banker will parade before you about four or five of his best men. You will probably not be working with these men, and you don't get a chance to see their full organization.

In the process of selection you might ask for an organization chart showing the number of people in each operation and go over it carefully. You will want to know the number of people in corporate finance and their capability. Many firms put on a good front in this area, but are actually very weak. You will want to discuss the firm's amount of capital and what it is used for besides investment banking. Investment banking is a risky business. A firm with plenty of capital can be more aggressive in pricing an issue and will have staying power if a bad year is encountered.

You will want to know whether the firm is well rounded with capability of doing any type of financing from private placements to public offerings and all special types of financing such as the sale of industrial revenue bonds, leasing, project financing, etc. You will want to weigh the advantages of having a firm which has its own distribution. You will want to know what financings the firm has done and may want to talk with the companies it has financed. And as we have said, even after having done all this, you may have a hard time making a choice.

If your company is sufficiently large you will have to decide whether to have one or more investment bankers and which firms complement each other best. One honest investment banker put it this way: "If my firm is your sole manager, you should only have one manager, but if my firm is not a manager, you should have another manager."

Your financial vice-president should deal separately with each investment banker that works for your company. In this way you get independent views and can compare one with the other. Your financial vice-president should be looking for depth of thinking and get rid of those that do not service your company with long range sound philosophy as well as proper detailed analysis.

Above all, you should not feel wedded to any firm. You are buying a service, and if the service ceases to be high quality you should look for another firm.

TAX AND ACCOUNTING CONSIDERATIONS

Obviously, with today's heavy burden of taxes, the effect on taxes of diferent financial maneuvers has to be carefully weighed. Your financial vice-president can't be expected to be a tax expert, but he should know when to call in an expert.

A top financial officer has to be much more than an accountant, but a strong background in accounting is a real asset.

Unfortunately, accountants don't like to accept the fact that there is a difference between keeping the books and analyzing them. When they try to get into financial analysis they may muddy the waters.

WHERE DO YOU FIND SUCH A FINANCIAL OFFICER?

We conclude this chapter with the thought that after reading it, you may wonder whether any financial vice-president would be sufficiently knowledgeable so that he could answer all of the questions we have raised. Probably not, but the questions may indicate to you the type of person your financial vice-president should be in order to cope with the problems that may arise for a large, multi-national corporation.

If you have come up through finance, you can handle the "overly clever" type of financial vice-president. But if you haven't, watch out for the financial "genius" without good judgment who is always coming up with the free lunch schemes which on the surface look so intriguing. Above all, what you want is a man with depth of judgment; he should not be swayed by the booms and busts. He will have to be firm in unpopular recommendations at times because he will have to counter short range considerations in order to help keep your company on an even keel over the long run.

Chapter 8

A SUMMARY:
PURPOSE OF FINANCE AND
CAPITAL MANAGEMENT

Finance and capital management are part of the overall management of a company and should help to achieve the principal purpose of a company. Therefore, before we make some concluding remarks on finance and capital management, we will state what we believe should be the purpose of a company from a financial point of view. It is:

TO SATISFY CONSUMERS' NEEDS IN A FREE COMPETITIVE MARKET ECONOMY, AND IN SO DOING, PAY FAIR COMPETITIVE WAGES AND PROVIDE, ON AVERAGE, AT LEAST A MINIMUM RETURN TO SATISFY INVESTORS FOR SUPPLYING THE CAPITAL—A RETURN BELOW THIS MINIMUM INDICATES THE MISDIRECTION OF CAPITAL—AND TO MAXIMIZE PROFITS ABOVE THE MINIMUM RETURN AS A REWARD FOR DOING SOMETHING BETTER FOR CONSUMERS THAN COMPETITORS.

In the introduction, we suggested that the broad goals that you might have for finance and capital management are:

1. Assure that outside capital will be available when it is needed for expansion at a reasonable cost.

167

2. Produce a satisfactory return on capital.

3. Have a satisfactory price for your stock.

We will finish up with a few basic comments and a statement of the purpose of finance and capital management which will help to assure that these goals will be achieved.

First, a few basic comments:

- Take a long-range view in making most financial decisions. Accept the fact that regardless of what your forecasts show, things can change in the future and your financing should be able to handle such changes.

- Work with your financial officer in establishing the three principal financial goals for your company and understand the reasons behind each one.

- Face the discipline that sound finance entails; forgo expansion if you cannot raise the capital on a sound basis. If you violate this rule, weigh the gamble you are taking and the possible consequences versus the potential return. Is it worth the risk?

- Keep your financing as simple as possible, so that it is easily understood by investors.

- Establish a sound dividend policy regardless of cash needs if your company is strong financially and can raise outside capital.

- Only spend capital that will provide an adequate return, whether it be by way of expansion or an acquisition.

- An acquisition should only be taken on if you can manage it and not as an investment. Keep your company in reasonably related lines in order to hold investor interest; investors can do their own diversifying.

- Keep investors informed about all the facts, both good and bad. And appreciate that too high a price for your stock may be as bad as too low since investors should receive a fair return; the price must be in keeping with your company's earning ability.

- Don't let your financial officer or some investment banker convince you that there is a free lunch in finance.
- Beware of those complicated computer runs that cover up truths which should be made simple to understand.
- A bad financial picture is either the result of unsound financial policy or inadequate earnings. If it is the former, it is poor financial management; if it is the latter, you may have wasted capital. Or, of course, you may have been hit by an Act of God outside of your control.

And finally, a statement of the purpose of finance and capital management:

TO TRANSFER THE SAVINGS OF OUR NATION IN AN ORDERLY FASHION INTO PRODUCTION SO AS TO PRODUCE MORE GOODS AND SERVICES WHICH CAN BE SOLD AT PRICES THAT WILL RESULT IN A RETURN AT LEAST SUFFICIENT TO SATISFY THE INVESTORS WHO PUT UP THE CAPITAL.

Thus, from raising capital from investors to finally rewarding investors fairly is a closed circle which should all tie together.

And a final word about our free enterprise system. Next to Democracy free enterprise is our country's greatest asset. It is misunderstood by the general public and, in fact, looked on with suspicion. Many things are needed to change this situation, including proper conduct by government and unions and education of everyone about how free enterprise works. However, above all, top executives must present a respectable image, and as far as finance is concerned they should shun the type of manipulations practiced by some of the conglomerates in the 1960s. Our free enterprise system needs true business statesmen whose aim is to make free enterprise have a universal appeal over any other system.

Appendices

EXAMPLES OF
CALCULATIONS OF RATES OF
RETURN ON INVESTMENT
FOR COMPANY
PERFORMANCE MEASURE,
DIVISION PERFORMANCE
STANDARDS AND PROJECT
PROFITABILITY ANALYSIS

Part I

Financial Statements to Represent Company Results Used in the Three Examples in Parts II, III and IV

Balance Sheet

Current assets	$100	Current liabilities		$50
Plant, net	50	Long-term capital		
		Debt	$27	
		Common	73	
		Total		$100
Total	$150	Total		$150

Income Statement

Sales	$200.00
Operating expenses	178.86
Income before interest and income taxes	$ 21.14
Interest	2.16
Income after interest before income taxes	$ 18.98
Income taxes at 50%	9.49
Net income	$ 9.49

Part II

**Company Performance Measure-
to Investor Rate**

The rate to be achieved is calculated as follows:

Debt	27%	× 8%	2.16
Common	73	× 13	9.49
Total	100%		11.65%

The company's results to compare with this ratio are derived from the financial statements in Part I as follows:

Income

Interest	$2.16
Net income	9.49
Total	$11.65

Long-term capital

Debt	$27
Common	73
Total	$100

$$\text{Return on total long-term capital} = \frac{\text{Total income}}{\text{Total long-term capital}}$$

$$= \frac{\$11.65}{\$100}$$

$$= \$11.65\%$$

Note: Interest is not adjusted for the effect of tax savings in either the rate to be achieved or in the income statement.

Part III

Division Performance Standards—Pre-Tax Rate

The rate to be achieved is calculated before income taxes as follows:

Debt	27% × 8%	2.16
Common 73 × 13		9.49
Total	100%	11.65
Income taxes at 50%		9.49
Pre-tax rate		21.14%

This rate, which is calculated on long-term capital, has to be adjusted so it can be applied to the asset side for division performance standards.

$$\frac{\text{Long-term capital}}{\text{Total assets}} \times \text{Rate} = \frac{\$100}{\$150} \times 21.14\%$$
$$= 14.09\%$$

This rate when applied to total assets will produce the proper rate on long-term capital.

The results to compare with this rate are derived from the financial statements in Part I as follows:

$$\frac{\text{Income before interest \& taxes}}{\text{Total assets}} = \frac{\$ 21.14}{\$150.}$$
$$= 14.09\%$$

Part IV

Project Profitability—
After Tax Equivalent Rate

The rate to be achieved is calculated as follows:

Debt	27% × 4% (after 50% tax rate)	1.08
Common	73 × 13	9.49
Total	100%	10.57%

This rate which is calculated on long-term capital has to be applied to an asset base.

$$\frac{\text{Long-term capital}}{\text{Total assets}} \times \text{Rate} = \frac{\$100}{150} \times 10.57\%$$
$$= 7.05\%$$

The results of a project which compares with this rate are derived from financial statements in Part I as follows:

Income before interest and taxes	$21.14
Income taxes (50%) with no interest deduction	10.57
Income after taxes	$10.57

$$\text{Return on total assets} = \frac{\text{Income after income taxes (with no reduction of taxes because of interest)}}{\text{Total assets}}$$

$$= \frac{\$10.57}{\$\ 150}$$

$$=\qquad 7.05\%$$

The reason the calculations have to be made this way for project profitability analysis is because the forecast income for a project is after taxes, but there is no reduction in taxes because of interest charges. This is so because in project profitability analysis the calculations do not include any interest. Therefore, to make the rate to be achieved comparable it is reduced by the tax savings which interest produces.

The figures for the project profitability rate can be reconciled as follows:

Project income after income taxes
without any tax savings from interest $10.57
When the project is integrated with the company
and capital is raised to finance the project with
27% debt, interest charges will reduce taxes
(2.16 x 50%) 1.08

After tax income before interest charges.......................... 11.65
Interest 2.16

Income for common ....$ 9.49

Appendix II

DISCOUNTING—
ITS MEANING

When your officers show you a forecast for a project, there will be outflows of capital, or in other words capital investment, and there will be inflows as a result of earnings. Because money has a time value, the inflows and outflows in the early years are worth more than flows in future years. Discounting merely provides a return on investment giving effect to the time value of money. So, project profitability analysis to be meaningful has to be done on a discounted basis.

You understand what compounding means. A dollar invested today at 10% interest will amount to $1.10 at the end of one year, and will amount to $1.21 at the end of two years with annual compounding. The compounding factors are 1.10 for year one and 1.21 for year two. Thus:

Year	Investment	Compounding Factor	Application	Compound
0	$1	1.10	$1 x 1.10	$1.10
1		1.21	1 x 1.21	1.21

Compounding shows what an original investment will be worth some time in the future at a certain rate.

Discounting is merely the reverse of compounding. It shows what a certain amount of money in the future is worth today. The discounting factors are the reciprocals of the compounding factors.

For example, what is $1.10 worth today if it is due in one year assuming an interest rate of 10%? It would be calculated as follows:

$$\$1.10 \ \times \ \frac{1}{1.10} \ = \ \$1.00$$

Thus, you would be willing to pay $1 today if you could get $1.10 in one year at a 10% rate because $1 invested today at 10% would produce $1.10.

The discount factors, as we have said, are the reciprocals of the compounding factors; that is 1/1.10 or .909. In other words, $1.10 times .909 equals $1, the present value of $1.10 in one year at 10%.

The discount factor for the second year at 10% would be 1/1.21 or .8264. Multiplying $1.21 times .8264 equals $1.00, the present value of $1.21 in two years at 10%.

There are various methods of discounting. One is called the internal rate of return, which gives a rate for the project. This rate is the discount rate which equalizes the present value of future inflows to the amount of the initial investment outflow. Another method, the present value technique, uses a certain rate for the investment and shows the excess or deficit in dollars with that assumed rate applied.

There are some technical problems in making the calculations, but your officers involved in project profitability analysis should be able to handle them.

What you really have to worry about is that the forecast used in calculating the return makes sense.

Appendix III

ACQUISITION PRICING—
RETURN ON
INVESTMENT APPROACH

An acquisition is a capital investment like putting money into plant and equipment. You merely do it by purchasing the ownership of the plant and equipment. The principal basis for making the decision as to whether to buy or not has to be return on capital. You would be disregarding your stockholders if you did not have this foremost in mind.

Furthermore your decision has to be made on prospective earnings. It is future earnings that you will receive, not past earnings. Therefore, you cannot avoid making a forecast.

Because of the unreliability of forecasts, you may feel that looking at future earnings is a waste of time. However, when you make an acquisition you are automatically forecasting, because if you decide to go ahead you have to be saying to yourself that future earnings will give an adequate return or otherwise you would turn it down.

The purpose of a forecast should be to answer two questions:

1. What profits have to be achieved to justify the price?
2. Is it conceivable that those profits can be achieved?

And to answer these questions you have to work with some figures. A simple way to look at the end result, which is drawn up from a forecast income statement and balance sheet, is shown in the exhibit to follow.

It shows the returns that will be earned on the acquisition and what has to be earned on tangible book value to achieve these earnings. These figures may help you decide whether attaining these profits is a reasonable expectation.

It also shows how long it will take to achieve a breakeven rate.

No matter what method of valuation you use you cannot avoid the problem of terminal value. This simple approach gives you a required terminal value to break even so that you can ask yourself whether such a terminal value makes sense.

We used the common cost rate for illustrative purposes. In your calculations you should use the profit goal rate you anticipate for the acquisition. And you will probably want to carry out the forecast 10 years.

Of course, there may be numerous adjustments that have to be made in order to compile these figures. For example, the figures have to be adjusted for a sound capital structure which may mean an addition to or subtraction from the common equity purchase price. And adjustments have to be made for any cash outflows or any additional common equity that is required.

However, this method of summarizing the final results may be helpful to obtain a broad view of the picture in order to answer the two questions we suggested above.

Breakeven Point for Acquisition—Year in Which Income Sufficient to Cover Common Cost

Line		Year 1	Year 2	Year 3	Year 4	Year 5
1	Forecast income available for common	$15	$20	$26	$33	$41
	Common book value at beginning of year[1]					
2	Excluding intangibles	$100	$115	$135	$161	$194
3	Including intangibles (purchase price)	157	172	192	218	251
	Return on beginning common book value					
4	Excluding intangibles	15.0%	17.4%	19.3%	20.5%	21.1%
5	Including intangibles (purchase price)	9.6	11.6	13.5	15.1	16.3
6	Required earnings—13% annual return times Line 3.	$20.41	$22.36	$24.96	$28.34	$32.63
7	Annual earnings (deficit) or surplus—Line 1 less Line 6.	(5.41)	(2.36)	1.04	4.66	8.37
8	Cumulative earnings (deficit) or surplus compounded at 13%.	(5.41)	(8.47)	(8.53)	(4.98)	2.74
9	Required terminal value to break even. Purchase price compounded at 13%.	$157.00	$177.41	$200.47	$226.53	$255.98[2]

Notes:

Assumptions for the above example:

    (a) Cost of common equity is 13%.

182

(b) All earnings are reinvested in the acquisition and no additional capital is required.

(c) Terminal value is equal to book value, including intangibles.

Adjustments have to be made in the purchase price if adjustments have to be made in the common equity to provide the appropriate amount of debt in the capital structure. Adjustments also have to be made in the forecast for any other additions to or reductions in common equity.

[1]Obtained by adding forecast income available for common for previous year to previous year beginning book value.

[2]Required terminal value is 6x forecast earnings, and 132% of tangible book value.

STOCK PRICE FORMULA

DEVIATIONS AND LIMITATIONS

Part I

**Formulas for Determining Price-Earnings Ratio and
Market Price Divided by Common Book Value**

DETERMINATION OF PRICE-EARNINGS RATIO FROM
DIVIDEND PAYOUT RATIO AND DIVIDEND YIELD

<u>Line</u>

Since

1 Dividend Payout Ratio $\quad = \dfrac{\text{Dividends per Share}}{\text{Earnings per Share}}$

2 and Dividend Yield $\quad = \dfrac{\text{Dividends per Share}}{\text{Market Price}}$

Then

$$3 \quad \frac{\text{Dividend Payout Ratio}}{\text{Dividend Yield}} \quad = \quad \frac{\dfrac{\text{Dividends per Share}}{\text{Earnings per Share}}}{\dfrac{\text{Dividends per Share}}{\text{Market Price}}}$$

$$4 \quad\quad\quad = \quad \frac{\text{Dividends per Share}}{\text{Earnings per Share}} \times \frac{\text{Market Price}}{\text{Dividends per Share}}$$

$$5 \quad\quad\quad = \quad \frac{\text{Market Price}}{\text{Earnings per Share}}$$

$$6 \quad\quad\quad = \quad \text{Price-Earnings Ratio}$$

DETERMINATION OF MARKET PRICE DIVIDED BY COMMON BOOK VALUE FROM RETURN ON COMMON BOOK VALUE AND PRICE-EARNINGS RATIO

Since

$$7 \quad \frac{\text{Return on Comnon}}{\text{Book Value}} \quad = \quad \frac{\text{Earnings per Share}}{\text{Common Book Value}}$$

$$8 \quad \text{and Price-Earnings Ratio} \quad = \quad \frac{\text{Market Price}}{\text{Earnings per Share}}$$

Then

$$9 \quad \frac{\text{Return on Common Book}}{\text{Value x Price-Earnings Ratio}} = \frac{\text{Earnings per Share}}{\text{Common Book Value}} \times \frac{\text{Market Price}}{\text{Earnings per Share}}$$

$$10 \quad\quad\quad = \quad \frac{\text{Market Price}}{\text{Common Book Value}}$$

Part II

Limitations of Formulas

1. They assume constant figures for price-earnings ratio, dividend payout ratio and increase in earnings from plowback.

    These figures are not constant for a particular company. Therefore, we have to use representative average figures.

2. They do not differentiate between return from dividends and market appreciation. Dividends are far more certain than the prospects of market appreciation. A lower overall return may be acceptable to some investors if a substantial portion of it comes in the form of dividend yield.

3. They cannot be used for a company which pays no dividends. In such a situation, no matter what the price-earnings ratio, the return to investors from market appreciation would be equal to the growth rate in earnings per share provided the price-earnings ratio remained constant.

4. The price-earnings ratio is overly sensitive when the price-earnings ratio is high and the dividend yield low. For example if the dividend payout ratio is 30% and the yield 2%, the price-earnings ratio would be 15x. If the yield were 1% the price-earnings ratio would double to 30x.

5. The price-earnings ratio is also sensitive to assumptions about the return required by investors. For example, if in the figures we have used, investors were satisfied with a 12% return rather than a 13% return, the required yield would decrease from 5.5% to 4.5% and the price-earnings ratio would increase from 7.7x to 9.3x.

6. In determining the return which stockholders receive, no allowance is made for any return on the dividend income. This would not change the results materially. Furthermore, we do not believe that investors make such a calculation in determining their total returns.

Note: Other more complicated formulas are available for the evaluation of stock prices which try to cope with some of the limitations of our approach.

INDEX

A

B

C

D

L

M

O